Scripture Union
Bible Guide

Scripture Union

Bible Guide

Scripture Union

47 Marylebone Lane London W1M 6AX

Text and the majority of the illustrations are copyright Scripture Union London.

Permission to use any part should be requested from:
Scripture Union, 47 Marylebone Lane, London W1.

ISBN 0 85421 726 6 (Bound into Bible)

ISBN 0 85421 727 4 (Separate Guide)
Illustrations by Annie Vallotton, Harold T. King, Stan Knight, Archie Mason, John Pickering.

Some background illustrations: Copyright Leif Stegeland Förlag AB Gothenburg, Sweden
Cover picture, Good News Bible: Dumb-bell Nebula in *Vulpecula*, copyright by the California Institute of Technology and the Carnegie Institution of Washington, 1961. Reproduced by permission from the Hale Observatories. Cover design by Roger Chouler.

Printed in England

Contents

Our opening section covers a vast period of human history, selecting key events. It provides a guide for what can easily be puzzling. Each double page deals with a period of time, and the approximate dates are given. Varied background facts, above and below the jigsaw pieces, help to give a fuller picture of God's working in the lives and history of the peoples of the Bible.

Creation In the beginning God made the universe and all that is in it (*see* ➥ 1). He created it all to a plan. The fact of creation is important because it tells clearly: ● the universe did not come into being by accident: it was created by God for a purpose ● everything was created good ● the crowning act was the creation of man ● human beings were distinct from the rest of creation because they were made as God's representatives to care for creation on his behalf ● that the greatest thing in it does not deserve worship: this should be reserved for the Creator alone.

The fall People were created perfect – complete and whole in every way, with freedom to choose to love God or not to love him. When they chose to go their own way they broke their wonderful relationship with God, with each other and with nature (*see* ➥ 2). This loss of rightness with God and the world is called – 'the fall'.

1 God makes the universe (Gen 1,2)　　**2** Everything goes wrong (Gen 3)　　**3** Noah and the flood (Gen 6.1–22)　　**4** God's promise to Abraham (Gen 12.1–9; 13.16; 15.5,6)　　**5** A wife for Isaac (Gen 24)　　**6** Jacob deceives his father, Isaac (Gen 27.1–29)

Other flood stories As civilization developed it was marked by idolatry, violence and excess. Then came 'the flood', of which there are many accounts. The one from Babylon is very similar to the *Genesis* narrative.

Noah's boat The boat God told Noah to build (133m × 22.25m × 13.4m) was big enough to hold 432 double-decker buses. In other words, there was plenty of room for the 35,000 or so animals that were saved from the flood with Noah and his family (*see* ➥ 3).

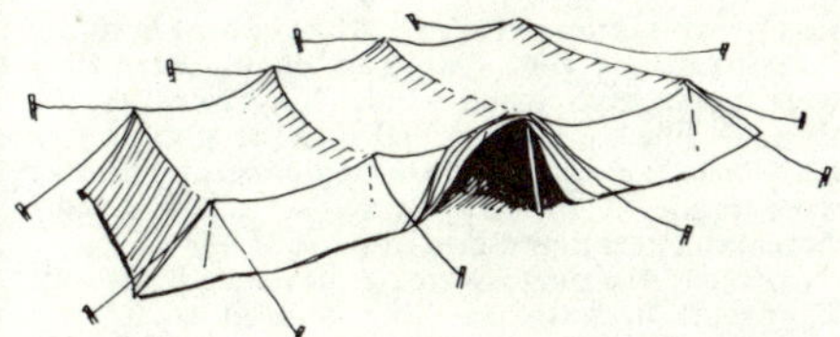

Tents In the days of Abraham, his family and relations lived in tents and were mainly shepherds, moving from place to place for pasture and water.

Usually made of goat-hair, most tents had nine poles, with three tall poles in the centre, and three shorter poles on each side. Modern Bedouin tents have changed very little from those of earliest times.

Egyptian writing The Egyptians used pictures as a means of writing. These were called hieroglyphs. 'Water' was written with three wavy lines ≈ and 'sun' with two circles – one inside the other – ◉ . As time went on the hieroglyphs were developed into the world's first alphabet signs.

In 1799, Napoleon's soldiers found a black stone at Rosetta in the Nile Delta. This stone had on it both the hieroglyphs and the Greek alphabet. Since scholars already knew the Greek they could decipher the hieroglyphs and find out their meaning.

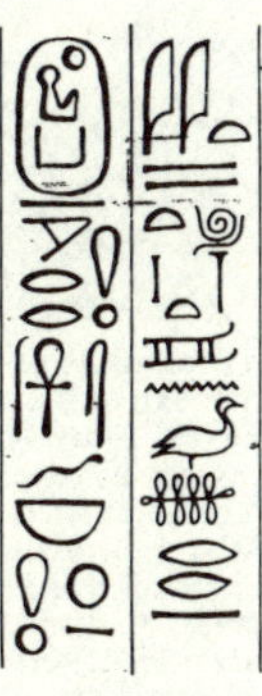

7 Jacob's dream at Bethel (Gen 28.10–22)   **8** Jacob is told that Joseph is dead (Gen 37.12–36)   **9** Two dreams of the king of Egypt (Gen 41.14–32)   **10** Joseph welcomes his family to Egypt (Gen 45.1—46.8)

Wells These were needed because rivers and streams often dried up in the hot dry summers. Quarrels sometimes broke out over ownership and who had the right to use them. Women had to draw the water for everybody in the family *and* for the animals.

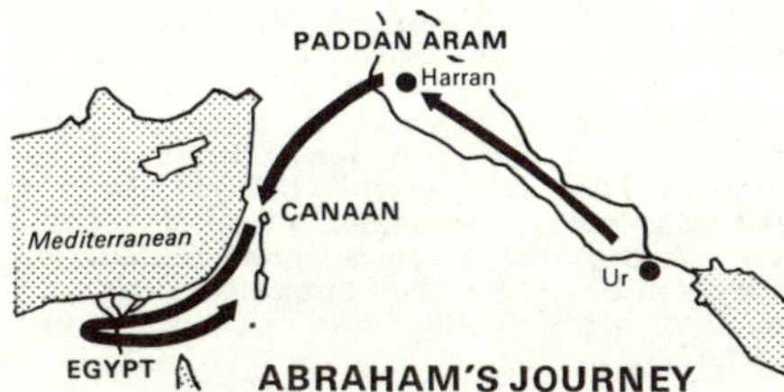

Birthright The eldest son had many privileges in the family: he succeeded his father as the family's head; was in charge of his brothers and sisters when the father was away from home; inherited twice as much as any other son; and received his father's dying words of blessing. Esau gave up his right to all these privileges when he light-heartedly exchanged them with his brother Jacob for some bread and soup.

Don't forget. Check with the index (*pages 57–63*) for more details on all subjects and Bible references.

Ten disasters of Egypt – (*Exodus chapters 7–12*)
God spoke of bringing justice against all the gods of Egypt. Since the Egyptian gods were thought to have been bound up with the forces of nature, each disaster was an attack on their power.

1 Water into blood; 2 frogs; 3 gnats; 4 flies; 5 death of the animals; 6 boils on people and animals; 7 destruction by hail; and 8 locusts; 9 darkness covers the land; and, lastly, 10 death of the firstborn.

Egyptian slave-drivers Although, at first, the Israelites were very happy in Egypt, later they were persecuted when a new king came to the throne. They were reduced to a slave class (*see illus: men working under a slave-driver*.) Bricks were made from clay, straw or stubble, and water; then set in moulds and dried.

Various disasters were experienced by all Egyptians because the king refused to let the Israelites leave Egypt. But, after the death of his firstborn child, he finally relented and, in triumph, Moses led God's people out of slavery.

1 A plan to keep Moses alive (Ex 2.1–10)　2 God speaks to Moses (Ex 3)　3 Disasters strike Egypt (Ex 7.14—12.42)　4 Death passes over the Israelites (Ex 12.1–36)　5 Escape from the enemy (Ex 14)　6 Ten commandments from God (Ex 20.1–17)

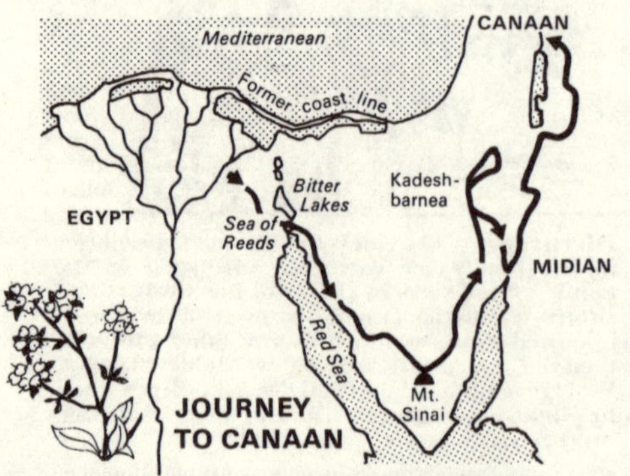

Passover The Jews still celebrate the festival of the Passover. They remember the night when death 'passed over' the Israelite homes whose doorposts had been smeared with blood (*see* 4). A sprig of a small bushy plant called hyssop (*see illus. on left*) was dipped in the blood of a lamb or young goat that had been specially selected. Then the blood was put as a sign on the doorposts of the homes of the Hebrews.

A meal of lamb – to remind them of God's provision – is still part of the Jewish Passover celebrations. The meat is roasted whole and a bowl of salt water put on the table as a reminder of the tears shed by the Israelites during the days of slavery in Egypt. A dish of bitter herbs brings to mind the hardship of the forty years spent living in the desert.

Covenant This important word is used to describe the special relationship God had with the people he chose. God made certain promises to his people and they committed themselves to worship and obey him in return, showing by their lives together what God is like and does.

Important covenants were made by God with Abraham, Moses and David. Many of the promises made then are fulfilled in Jesus. So Christians are called 'The people of the new covenant'.

Ark (Box) of the Covenant The Covenant Box (measuring 110 centimetres long, 66 centimetres wide and 66 centimetres high) was made of hard acacia wood and covered inside and out with gold. On the lid were two winged creatures made of gold, facing each other. These were probably strange, powerful creatures with symbolic meaning.

Tent of the Lord's Presence While the Israelites were journeying through the desert to Canaan and living in tents, they had a special tent (*tabernacle*) in which they worshipped God. It reminded them that God was always with his people.

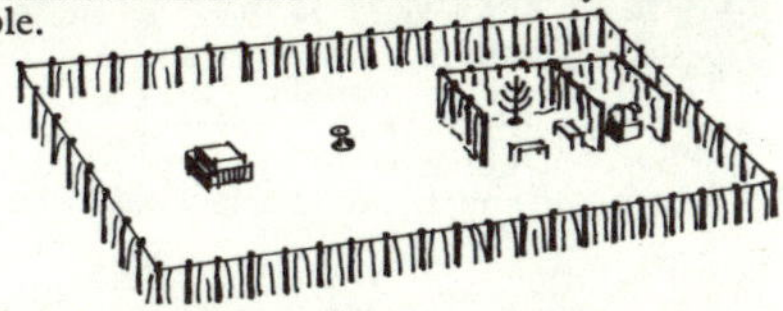

1060 BC

7 Moses hands over to Joshua (Deut 31.1–8) 8 Marching round Jericho (Josh 6) 9 Gideon offers a sacrifice (Judg 6.25–32) 10 Naomi gains a grandson (Ruth 4.13–17) 11 God calls Samuel (1 Sam 3)

Canaanite religion The people who lived in Canaan practised fertility worship and especially honoured the Master (i.e. Baal) and his Mistress. The sex organs were revered, and priests and priestesses were available in their temples for sexual intercourse which was seen as worship. To those Israelites who were faithful to God this was idolatry; to others it had a powerful attraction.

The judges (or liberators) For almost two hundred years, between the death of Joshua and the rise of Samuel, God gave the Israelites military leaders who freed them from their enemies. This period of Israel's history followed a depressing pattern: the Israelites turned from trusting God and began to worship the gods of Canaan; they copied the lifestyle of the people of Canaan which included many forbidden and unjust practices. As a consequence, God allowed them to be defeated by their enemies but, when they cried to him for help, he sent them a liberator (*deliverer or judge*), to free them and bring them back to justice. A short time of prosperity followed – then the pattern started all over again.

Don't forget. Check with the index (*pages 57–63*) for more details on all subjects and Bible references.

Sacrifice Sacrifices are mentioned very early in the Bible. Sometimes they were thank-offerings (as in the case of Noah), but the people also realized that they needed God's forgiveness. When they gave an animal offering to God they were giving up something of their own and saying sorry for the wrong in their lives.

At first, the head of the family offered sacrifices to God on an altar – a kind of 'table' on which a fire was lit to roast the sacrifice – but later Moses appointed Aaron and his descendants as priests to do this task.

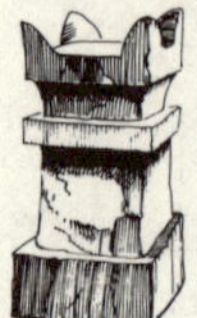

Altars Men of God, such as Abraham, Isaac and Jacob, often built altars at a place where they heard the voice of God. They were used for sin or thank-offerings of animals, birds or grain. The first altars were natural sites – a mound of earth, or a block of stone or rock. Later, the altars were more elaborate – carved rock or even covered with gold, and pieces called 'horns' were added at the four corners (*illus. left = limestone altar found at Megiddo, see its corner pieces*). A man who wanted God's protection would hold on to the horns of the altar.

1 Samuel anoints Saul (1 Sam 10) **2** David in Saul's court (1 Sam 16.14–23) **3** David defeats Goliath (1 Sam 17) **4** Jealousy of Saul in action (1 Sam 18.6–16) **5** Jonathan helps David (1 Sam 20) **6** David reveals his strategy (1 Sam 26)

Anointing Kings, prophets and priests (*e.g. Saul: see* ♣ 1), as well as the tent which represented God's presence and all its furniture, had olive oil poured on them to mark them out for special use for God. They were 'messiah-ed' (*Hebrew word*) or 'anointed'; the Greek would be 'christ-ed'.

Jesus was the 'Messiah' or 'Christ' – the anointed or specially chosen one of God.

Shepherds and sheep The many sheep in Israel were kept for their wool, for food and for sacrifice, whilst their skins provided leather. Most of them were cream and brown coloured. The rams' horns were used as trumpets or as holders of oil.

The shepherd, who often knew his sheep by name, did not drive them from behind but walked in front of them. He took great care of them: at night they were usually put into a sheepfold – an enclosure of dry-stone walls – about two metres high with no door, only an opening across which the shepherd lay.

The Philistines (*Philistine soldier with other captives*). By the time the Israelites entered Canaan, the Philistines had settled along the coastal strip between Egypt and Gaza. They were the chief rivals of the Israelites for many years. But, during David's reign, they became less of a danger and paid taxes to him and afterwards to Solomon.

Musical instruments David played a harp made of wood, strung with gut, and plucked with the fingers (*see* 2 4). He may have played the flute as well, for the boys often made simple pipes from reeds.

The trumpet, or ram's horn, cymbals, bells and the tambourine were also used in the worship of God.

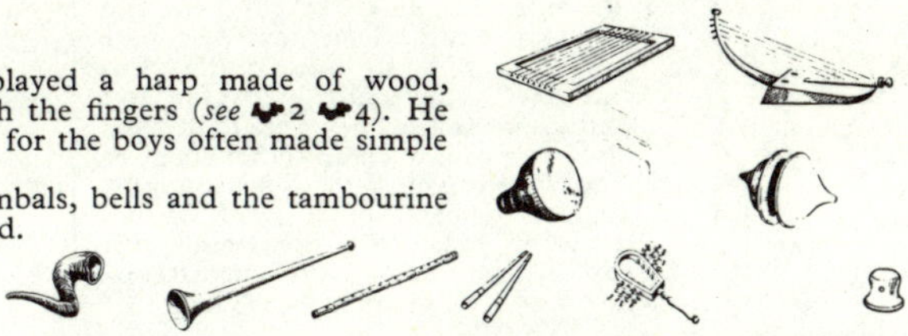

950 BC

7 David – king at last (2 Sam 5.1–12)   8 Solomon asks God for wisdom (1 Kgs 3.1–15)   9 Work starts on Solomon's Temple (1 Kgs 5)   10 A visit from the Queen of Sheba (1 Kgs 10.1–13)   11 Solomon builds temples for foreign gods (1 Kgs 11.1–13)

Solomon's Temple David wanted to build a permanent house where the people could worship God. He made very full plans for the building of a Temple, but, because many people had been killed in the battles he had fought against Israel's enemies, God did not allow him to go ahead. Instead, Solomon, his son, was given the job.

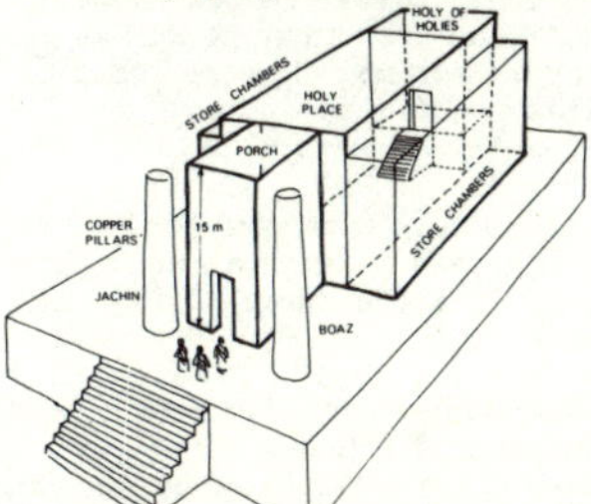

The best craftsmen were hired, and pine and cedarwood brought from Lebanon (*see* 9), though the actual preparations were not carried out on site (*see pages 48, 49*). Heavy taxation was introduced to pay for the work.

Trade Although Israel was a small unimportant country, its position as a natural bridge between Egypt and Babylon helped her to gain from the trade and commerce that went through the land. She was able to control the trade routes and force those using them to share their profits with her.

Her own exports included grain, oil and wine, as well as wool. Trade prospered under David and Solomon, owing to the conquests of David and Solomon's many marriages with foreign princesses and alliances with their countries.

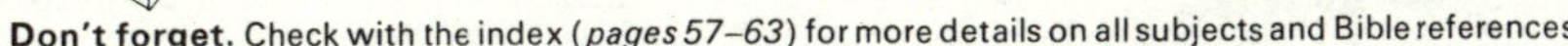

Don't forget. Check with the index (*pages 57–63*) for more details on all subjects and Bible references.

Israel and Judah Solomon's son, Rehoboam, was asked to lower the heavy taxes that his father had placed on the people. He refused and there was a revolt by ten of the tribes. With Jeroboam as their leader, they started a rival kingdom – sometimes known as 'the northern kingdom'. It kept the name of Israel. Two new places of worship were set up – one in the north and one in the south – at Dan and Bethel (*see* ⟿ 2). They were to become places for idol worship rather than for true worship of God. The southern kingdom, Judah – made up of the two tribes of Judah and Benjamin, with part of the tribe of Levi – had Rehoboam, son of Solomon, as its king.

Prophets of Israel		
	Prophet	King
9th century	Elijah	Ahab
	Elisha	Ahab – Jehoash
8th century	Jonah	Jeroboam II
	Amos	Jeroboam II
(came from Judah, but prophesied in Israel)		
	Hosea	Jeroboam II
	?Joel	Joash
Prophets of Judah		
8th century	Isaiah	Uzziah – Hezekiah
	Micah	Jotham – Hezekiah

1 Division of the kingdom foretold (1 Kgs 11.27–39)   **2** Israel turns from God (1 Kgs 12.25–33)   **3** Ravens bringing food to Elijah (1 Kgs 17.1–7)   **4** God shows his power (1 Kgs 18.20–40)   **5** Murder for a vineyard (1 Kgs 21)   **6** Elisha takes over (2 Kgs 2.6–13)

Vineyard Vines, a frequent sight in Israel, were usually grown in terraces. The vineyard was very carefully prepared, often taking as long as three years to develop. Thorny hedges were often planted to keep out animals, and at harvest time a watchman stayed in a stone tower to protect the grapes from thieves.

Building Poor people built their own houses, using stone or clay bricks, dried in the sun. But large building projects employed skilled stone-masons, carpenters and craftsmen, as well as un-skilled labourers and porters: all were under the close watch of a master builder.

A plumb-line (*see* ⟿ 9) was used to check that the walls were straight.

Skin-diseases *Leviticus* (*chapters 13 and 14*) sets out what people had to do if a minor skin-disease developed into the more serious and dreaded complaint.

Severe cases often had to move away from their homes, and, if they came near other people, had to wear torn clothes and call out 'unclean' as a warning. They were not thought of as unclean because of contagion but because contact with

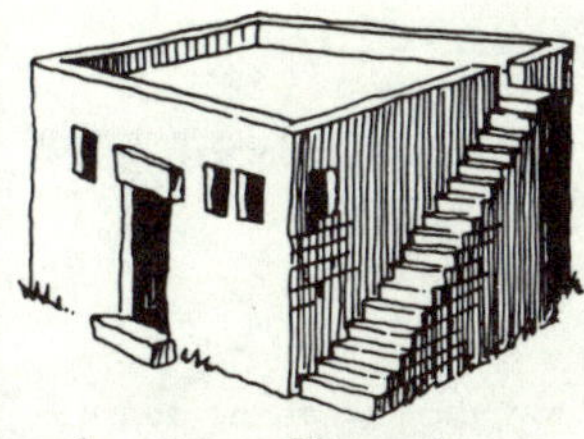

Houses There were fine houses as well as ordinary homes. Some houses were built on to caves to make them larger; others, built of clay bricks, only had one room with space on a slightly lower level for storing food for the family and animals – and even the beasts themselves in winter and war-time. Flat roofs were used for storage, for drying fruit or grain, for children playing and for eating and sleeping in the summer. Windows were small and few, so that it was easier to keep the house warm in winter and cool in summer. Glass was not yet used, and very little wood, though rich homes often had carved wood to decorate the walls and ceilings.

7 Send for Elisha! (2 Kgs 4.18–37)   **8** A slave girl helps Naaman (2 Kgs 5)   **9** God tells Amos that Israel is like a wall out of line (Amos 7.7–9)   **10** Hosea is used to show God's love to his people (Hos 3 ; see also 2.19–23)   **11** Isaiah's warning is uncomfortable! (Isa 28.14–21)   **12** The fall of Samaria (2 Kgs 17.5–23)

them caused others to be 'unclean' in the eyes of God, and therefore unable to take part in public worship. If the skin healed, it had to be examined by a priest, and a thanksgiving offering made to God.

Clothes

(a) *Men's clothes* Most people dressed simply in either knee or ankle-length tunics, with or without sleeves. These were made of wool or linen, and over them was worn a long cloak, which was normally taken off for work and used for keeping warm at night. Head cloths were usually bound with a cord. Poor people mostly went bare-foot, but sandals, when worn, were taken off inside the house.

(b) *Women's clothes* These were very similar to men's clothing, but made of finer material and more colourful. A simple dress, often with an embroidered panel at the neck and a sash at the waist, was the main garment; a cap, decorated with coins and covered with a long veil, was worn on the head. For special occasions women liked to wear jewels and gold.

Don't forget. Check with the index (*pages 57–63*) for more details on all subjects and Bible references.

Assyria During the eighth century BC, Assyria became a very powerful nation (see ➤ 1). Its borders were extended as neighbouring territories were attacked and defeated. The defeated nations were forced to pay taxes of money and goods, and captives were taken from their countries back to Assyria. Israel's capital, Samaria, was defeated in 722 BC after a three-year siege. This was the end of the northern kingdom.

Sennacherib's inscription Sennacherib, a powerful Assyrian king (705–681 BC), tells how he besieged Jerusalem and threatened King Hezekiah.

1 Assyria threatens Jerusalem (2 Kgs 18, 19) **2** Josiah and the lost book (2 Kgs 22.8–20) **3** Jehoiakim destroys Jeremiah's scroll (Jer 36.20–26) **4** Jeremiah writes another scroll (Jer 36.27–32) **5** Captives being taken to Babylon (2 Kgs 25.8–12) **6** Amazing experience for Ezekiel (Ezek 37.1–14)·

Josiah and the lost book Josiah (640–609 BC), one of the kings of Judah who pleased God, tried to encourage the people to worship him properly. Idols were destroyed throughout the land and removed from the Temple. The neglected Temple was repaired, and while this was being done a scroll of the Law was found (see ➤ 2). When it was read to the people, they realized how much they had disobeyed God's laws.

The Samaritans When Samaria was defeated by the Assyrians (722 BC) the leading citizens were taken as captives to Assyria, and replaced with captives from other countries who did not believe in God. Intermarriage took place with the poorer Israelites of the northern kingdom who had been left behind and this mixed race became known as the Samaritans. When the Jews from the southern kingdom were allowed to return home, they despised the Samaritans because they were a mixed people and included many who did not believe in God; so they refused to allow them to help with the rebuilding of the Temple. The Jews and Samaritans were enemies well into New Testament times.

Babylon When the power of Assyria weakened (612 BC) the Babylonian empire took its place. Its most famous king was Nebuchadrezzar II (605–562 BC). Judah was conquered in 597 BC, when the king and all the leaders – including the prophet Ezekiel – the skilled craftsmen and all who were thought to be 'useful' were deported (see ❤5).

Babylon was a huge, magnificent city with a wall twenty-six metres thick and many marvellous gates and palaces. The streets were wide and lined with trees and the river Euphrates flowed through the city.

Nebuchadrezzar built the famous 'Hanging Gardens' (see right) for his wife.

7 Rescued from burning (Dan 3.8–30)   **8** A shock message (Dan 5.1–31)   **9** God saves Daniel (Dan 6)
10 Going home! (Ezra 1, 2)   **11** Rebuilding the Temple (Ezra 3.10, 11)   **12** Nehemiah overcomes opposition (Neh 4.1, 14–23; 6.15)

The Jews around the world Even before Israel and Judah were captured by Assyria and Babylon, God's people had settled in Syria and Egypt. But after these times the movement of the Jews increased and they travelled further afield (see map). Trade, commerce and military service all added to this, until, by New Testament times, more Jews lived outside Judaea than in it. They built their own local places of worship, and these became a stepping stone for Paul and the early missionaries of Jesus Christ.

Cylinder of Cyrus Cyrus, king of Persia, conquered Babylon (539 BC) and allowed any foreign captives who wished to return to their homes to do so. He gave the Jews help to rebuild Jerusalem and the Temple. A clay barrel, now in the British Museum (see illus.) tells of his battles and victories.

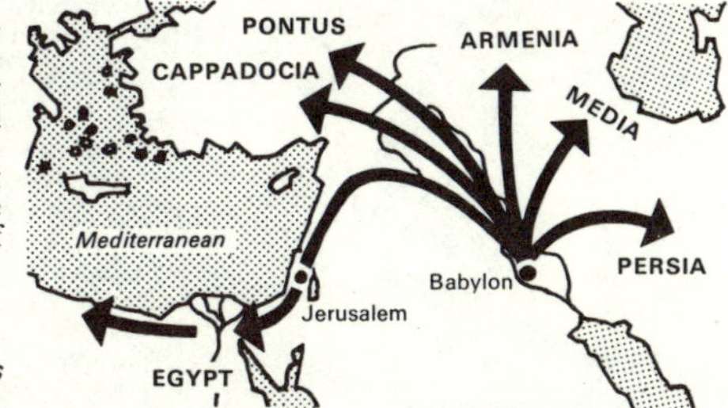

Map shows the areas where Jews settled

Don't forget. Check with the index (*pages 57–63*) for more details on all subjects and Bible references.

This period covers the time between the Old and New Testaments. The Bible does not give any details of these times but other history fills in some details.

Antiochus Epiphanes (175–163 BC) ⟨4⟩ Antiochus, a king of the Syrian empire, was the son of Antiochus the Great. He called himself 'Theos Epiphanes' (= '*god clearly shown*') claiming to be the Greek god, Zeus, in human form. The Jews nicknamed him 'Antiochus Epimanes' (= '*the mad man*'). In an effort to strengthen a tottering kingdom, he tried to spread Greek thought and way of life throughout his empire, including the worship of Greek gods.

In 168 BC he marched against Jerusalem, killing many of the Jews. The Temple was looted and many of its treasures stolen. He outraged the Jews when he put a statue of Zeus in the Temple and forced the Jewish priests to offer sacrifices of pigs (*unclean animals to the Jews*) on the Temple altar. Many Jews submitted to Antiochus, but the seeds of revolt were planted.

Alexander the Great (331–323 BC) ⟨1⟩ Alexander, king of Macedonia in Northern Greece, was a great soldier. His conquests extended from Greece to India and as far south as Egypt, where he founded the great city of Alexandria. His empire included Palestine, so once again this kingdom changed hands.

The Ptolemies and Seleucids (323–63 BC) ⟨2⟩ The empire of Alexander was divided up after his sudden death in 323 BC. Ptolemy, one of Alexander's generals, ruled Egypt, while Seleucus, another general, seized Babylonia and Asia Minor. There were constant battles between the two powers for control of Palestine. The Ptolemies of Egypt were to rule it for about a hundred years, then in 198 BC Antiochus the Great (*a descendant of Seleucus*) regained it for the Seleucids and Syrian rule until 63 BC.

Greek Old Testament ⟨3⟩ Alexandria, the capital of the Egypt of the Ptolemies, had a very large community of Jews who no longer spoke Hebrew. They wanted a Greek translation of their scriptures, and it is said that seventy-two scholars were sent from Jerusalem to complete this. It became known as the Septuagint (= '*seventy*'), sometimes written as LXX. To begin with, only the first five books of the Old Testament were included, but other books were added later.

Maccabean revolt (167 BC) ⟨5⟩ Rebellion broke out in the tiny village of Modein, not far from Jerusalem. An old priest, Mattathias, refused to obey an order to sacrifice to the Greek gods. He killed a Jew who was about to do so and the king's officer in charge of the sacrifices. His sons and followers took cover in the hills and gathered together an army of Jews willing to fight Antiochus and his men. For a time they were very successful and destroyed many altars to Greek gods. In 164 BC they were able to repair and rededicate the Temple to the worship of God.

One of the greatest leaders of the Maccabean revolt was Judas, the son of Mattathias, who was given the nickname 'Maccabeus' (= '*Hammerer*') because of his driving force and energy.

Pharisees ⟨6⟩ First called the Chasidim (=*'pious ones'*), this religious group of men supported the Maccabeans in the revolt against Antiochus. They studied both the Jewish Law (written Law), and the traditions that had been added to the Law (the spoken Law). They wanted to explain the Law to make it up-to-date and easier for the people to serve God properly. Some of them were very strict about following every little detail, and would rather die than fight on the sabbath. Later they were known as Pharisees (=*'separate ones'*). The descendants of the Maccabeans became priest-kings, and the Pharisees soon found they could not support these men and their ambition for great political power.

Sadducees ⟨6⟩ The party of Sadducees was small in number. Many of its members had come from priestly families and so objected to the descendants of the Maccabeans calling themselves priests; though in every other way they supported them and their successors. Their dislike of all change and a desire to keep everything as it was led to frequent quarrels with the Pharisees. The Sadducees rejected the additional rules and interpretations added by the Pharisees, and only recognized the Law of Moses (the written Law). They did not believe in life after death and the existence of angels and demons. They kept on good terms with the Romans when they came to power.

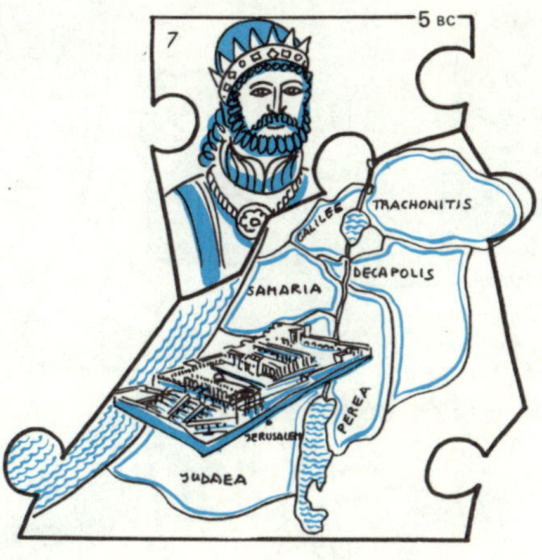

Augustus, Emperor of Rome (27 BC–AD 14) ⟨8⟩ Caesar Augustus became the first of the Roman emperors. His reign was noted for order and good government. But the countries under his rule had to pay heavy taxes to Rome. Some Jews agreed to be tax collectors, and for this betrayal they were treated as outcasts by their countrymen.

Herod's Temple ⟨7⟩ Herod was famous for his building projects and his heavy taxes. Although he was responsible for the erection of the third Temple in Jerusalem, the Jews still hated him. A thousand priests were trained to act as masons, and were the only ones allowed to work on the sacred site – even though there were ten thousand workmen altogether. The main structure of cream stone and gold was completed in ten years (9 BC), but the whole building was still unfinished in the time of Jesus.

It was finally destroyed by the Romans in AD 70, about six years after its completion.

Herod the Great and his kingdom ⟨7⟩ After a time of civil war the Jews were conquered by the Romans. With their support, Herod managed to conquer Idumea, Samaria, Galilee and Jerusalem. The last of the 'Maccabeans, Antigonus, was executed and Herod's kingdom was secure. Although Herod ruled sternly, his reign (40–4 BC) was free from war. When he died (4 BC) the kingdom was divided between his remaining sons: Archelaus, the eldest son, ruled Judaea, Samaria and Idumea; Galilee and Perea went to Antipas; and his north-eastern territories to Philip. But the rule of Archelaus was so harsh that he was finally banished by the Romans and replaced by a Roman Governor. Pontius Pilate was Governor at the time of Jesus.

Don't forget. Check with the index (*pages 57–63*) for more details on all subjects and Bible references.

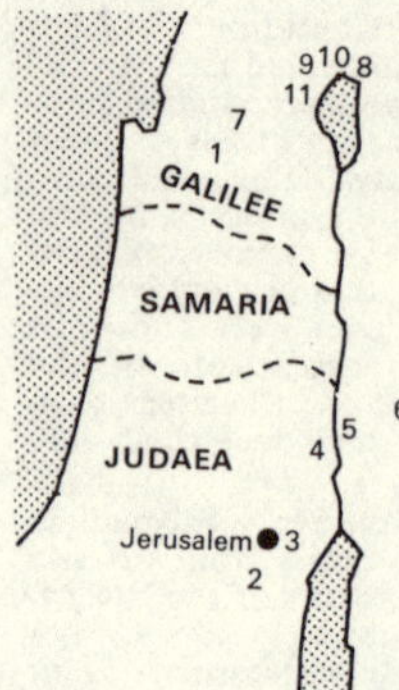

Locating map Check the numbered jigsaw pieces against the numbers of the map and notice how much Jesus travelled about.

Babies When a baby was born it was washed and wrapped in strips of cloth, about ten centimetres wide and five metres long. They were wound right round the baby's arms and legs, until it looked rather like a cocoon of a butterfly.

Angels The words translated angel simply mean messenger. Sometimes they refer to human messengers but usually to special spiritual beings who worship and serve God, care for his people and bring his messages to them.

Dating The first Christian calendar, dividing history into BC (*before Christ*) and AD (*anno domini* = '*in the year of the Lord*') was worked out by a monk in the sixth century AD. But it has now been found that he was about five years out in his calculations: so Jesus was born about 5 BC – and not AD 1 – towards the end of the reign of Herod the Great.

1 The birth of Jesus is announced (Lk 1.26–38) **2** Jesus is born (Lk 2.1–7) **3** The boy Jesus in the Temple (Lk 2.41–52) **4** Crowds listen to John the Baptist (Lk 3.2–18) **5** Jesus is baptized (Lk 3.21, 22)

Coming of age At the age of twelve or thirteen, a Jewish boy came of age and became a 'son of the Law'. He had to know the Law and commandments by heart and try to obey them. He could sit with the men in the synagogue (*see* 3) and wear a phylactery and prayer shawl.

A phylactery is a little black box worn by men when they pray. It is fastened by leather straps on the forehead or left arm; inside it there is a copy of some verses from the Law.

The synagogue When the people of Judah were captured and taken away from their homeland, they began to meet together in their homes on the sabbath (Saturday). Later, special buildings were erected called synagogues – a word which means 'gathering together'. By New Testament times every village had its own place for worshipping God. Every sabbath, and on festival days, the people met together for singing, prayers, readings from the Old Testament and discussion. The men could ask questions about the reading, or the Law, but the women, who sat on their own with the children, were not allowed to speak.

The Devil and demons The Bible shows that many of the spiritual beings created by God have turned against him. They are responsible for leading people away from God and are involved in the spread of sin, sickness, suffering and evil in the world. They are led by an evil being called Satan (a Hebrew word meaning 'accuser'), known also as the Devil and the Evil One.

God showed through the life, death, resurrection and ascension of Jesus Christ that the power of these evil beings is limited. Jesus defeated them and can help others to do the same.

Early learning Before the start of the synagogues, the children were educated by their parents. But by the time of Jesus most towns and villages had a synagogue school for children and adults. From the age of five or six, boys attended for religious instruction from teachers of the Law, while the girls stayed at home to be taught by their mothers how to cook and care for a family. Pupils learned by heart much of the Scriptures, especially the Law. Some learned to read the Old Testament, most of which was written in Hebrew.

6 The Devil tempts Jesus (Mt 4.1–11)   **7** Water into wine (Jn 2.1–11)   **8** Four fishermen follow Jesus (Mk 1.14–20)   **9** Peter's mother-in-law is healed (Lk 4.38,39)   **10** Paralysed man brought to Jesus (Mk 2.1–12)   **11** Jesus teaches about prayer (Mt 6.7–15)

John the Baptist John the Baptist was the second cousin of Jesus. Great crowds went to listen to him (see 4). He told them that they needed a complete change of direction in their lives, and that they must own up to and turn away from all the wrong things they had said and done. He made it plain that if they wanted to obey God and make a new start, then they should be baptized. He claimed that his task was to point out Jesus Christ as the specially chosen one of God.

The disciples of Jesus: Simon Peter, Andrew, James, John, Philip, Bartholomew (probably the surname of Nathanael), Thomas, Matthew (Levi), James (son of Alphaeus), Judas (Lebbaeus) whose surname was Thaddaeus, Simon (a member of the Jewish resistance movement), and Judas Iscariot (perhaps a member of the extremist group of 'dagger - men' pledged to kill Roman soldiers and officials).

Fishing In the time of Jesus there was a thriving fishing industry on the shores of Lake Galilee. At least four of the twelve disciples were fishermen – Peter, Andrew, James and John (see 8). The most usual way of fishing was with drag-nets (see illus.) but cast-nets, hooks and lines or a spear were also used.

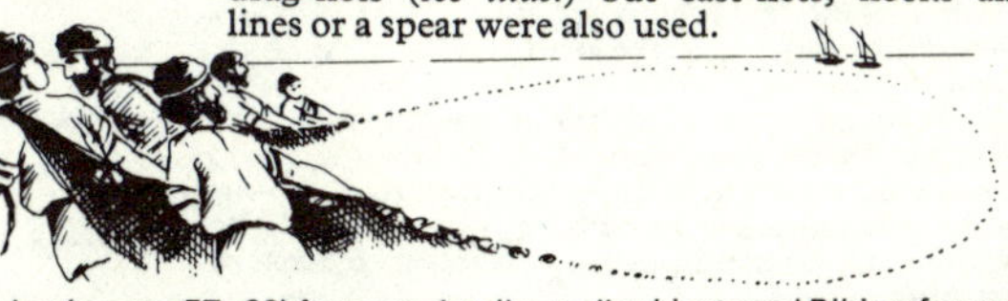

Don't forget. Check with the index (*pages 57–63*) for more details on all subjects and Bible references.

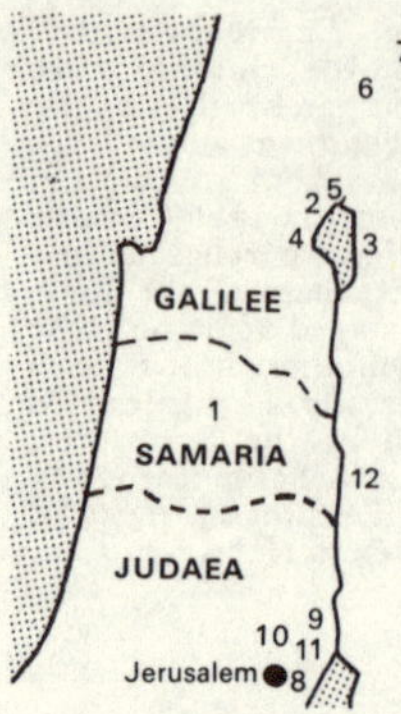

Keeping the Sabbath

The seventh day of the week was kept as a day of rest: no work was allowed. It lasted from sunset on Friday until sunset on Saturday. The day was intended for the good of men, women and children, giving them time to worship God and to enjoy some leisure. But so many detailed regulations had been added to God's rules for the sabbath that it became more of a burden than a day to look forward to.

Miracles

Jesus did many astonishing things – miracles or signs. The index (*pages 57–63*) gives a list. They show his power, his love for people and desire to help them.

The Gospel written by John records seven miracles, apart from the death and resurrection of Jesus. John chose particular miracles to help his readers to see Jesus as the Son of God and to show the necessity of trust in him.

Miracles in John
- Water turned into wine (*ch.2*)
- Healing of an official's son (*ch.4*)
- Healing of a lame man (*ch.5*)
- A great crowd fed (*ch.6*)
- Jesus walks on the water (*ch.6*)
- Healing of a blind man (*ch.9*)
- Lazarus brought back to life (*ch.11*)

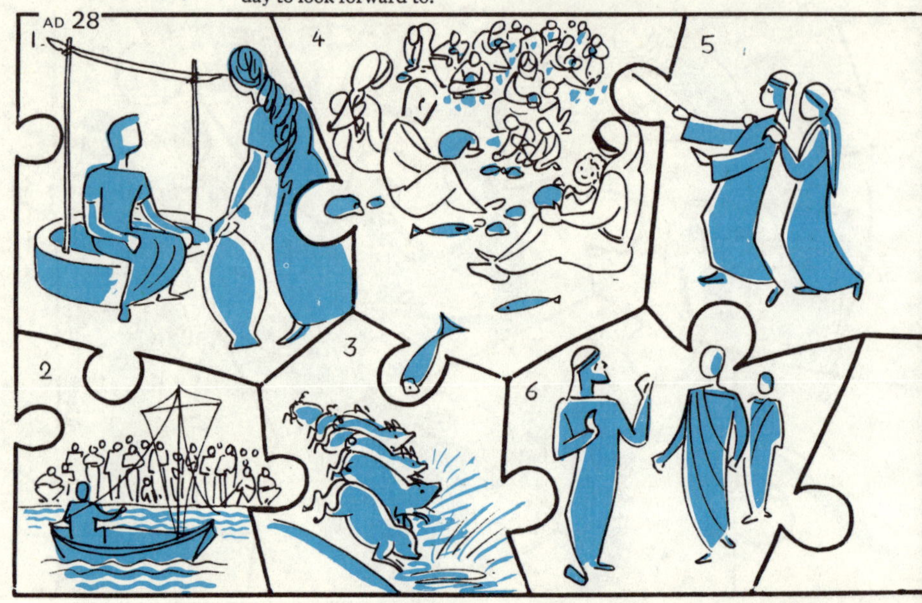

1 A meeting with a Samaritan woman (Jn 4.1–30) **2** Teaching from a boat (Mk 4) **3** Pigs destroyed by demons (Lk 8.26–39) **4** An unexpected meal (Mk 6.30–44) **5** Blind leaders are dangerous (Mt 15.10–14) **6** Peter tells the truth about Jesus (Mt 16.13–20)

Parables

One of the most frequent meanings of the word translated parable is 'something put alongside'. Parables are stories based on everyday life; they teach a particular truth.

There are different types of parables:
- *short sayings*, e.g. 'You are like light for the whole world' (*Matthew 5.14*).
- *longer sayings*, e.g. 'No one uses a piece of new cloth to patch up an old coat, because the new patch will shrink and tear off some of the old cloth, making an even bigger hole' (*Mark 2.21*).
- *complete stories*, e.g. the man sowing corn (*Luke 8.4–8*).

The parables divided the listeners into two groups: those who wanted to understand and those who were unwilling or uninterested. To the latter, the stories were baffling, but to those who wanted understanding they were a means of learning more.

Ploughing and sowing Many people worked on the land in Palestine. Various crops were grown, including wheat, barley, horse beans, lentils, onions, small cucumbers, marrows, water melons, figs, olives, grapes, pomegranates and dates. Ploughing began in autumn. A wooden plough was used, pulled by oxen yoked together. The seed was scattered by hand.

Food Most people had a very light breakfast of dried fruit and milk. Lunch for the poorer people would often be bread, fish and fruit. The women baked their own bread every day, and always took great care to prepare all their food according to the laws of Moses. (*See illus. – an oven made with a large clay dish*).

The main meal of the day was eaten in the evening. It might be meat or fish, vegetables and fruit. Many vegetables were eaten raw while the meat was boiled, but the lamb for the Passover meal had to be roasted. Meat was usually served on a large dish and eaten with the fingers. People drank wine, milk and water. The olive played an important part in diet, providing fruit and oil. Since there was no sugar, honey, dates, raisins and figs provided sweetenings.

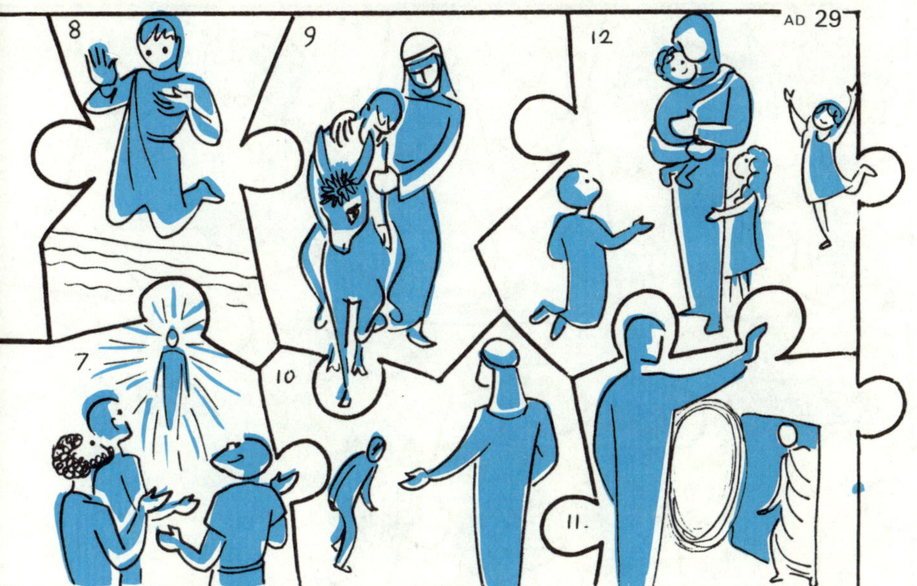

7 Jesus shows his glory (Mt 17.1–13)   **8** Blind man sees! (Jn 9)   **9** Love your neighbour (Lk 10.25–37)
10 Lost son returns home (Lk 15.11–32)   **11** Lazarus back from the dead (Jn 11.1–44)   **12** Jesus welcomes little children (Mk 10.13–15)

Games Children enjoyed many games similar to those played today: for instance, 'mothers and fathers' and 'weddings' and 'funerals'. Balls and pebbles, slings and stones – even bows and arrows – were all used in their games. Archaeologists have found board games and dice, babies' rattles and dolls.

The carpenter Every village had a carpenter/builder to make ploughs, yokes and other farm tools, as well as doors and household chests. An axe, a knife, a chisel and a saw were the tools of his trade, and, usually, he did the work of a stone mason, too. Often people skilled in the same craft lived in the same part of the town.

Don't forget. Check with the index (*pages 57–63*) for more details on all subjects and Bible references.

Hospitality To the Jew hospitality was very important. Even an unexpected visitor was always offered refreshment. A host was careful to greet his guests correctly. He would kiss them on arrival and again when they left. A servant would normally wash their feet which became very hot and tired on the dusty roads. Another way of showing pleasure on the guests' arrival, and to make them comfortable after a walk in the hot sun, was to put oil on their foreheads.

Festivals Various festivals or feasts were held each year. These were all celebrations of what God had done for his people at different times throughout their history. The most important festivals were: Shelters (*Tabernacles*) (*see pages 45 and 50, 51*), Passover (*see page 8*) and Harvest (*Pentecost*) (*see page 24*).

1 Joyful entry to Jerusalem (Mt 21.1–11) 2 Jesus clears the Temple (Mk 11.15–18) 3 The last supper (Lk 22.14–23) 4 Wash one another's feet (Jn 13.2–17) 5 Betrayed by Judas (Lk 22.47–53) 6 Just as Jesus said (Lk 22.54–62)

The last supper This meal that Jesus had with his disciples was at Passover time. The type of bread used had no yeast in it, so it was flat and 'pierced'. Jesus' body was pierced – but with a spear. He pointed to himself as the passover lamb, for his blood would bring deliverance from sin. As the wine was poured out, so his blood would be 'poured out' on the cross. Christians still celebrate this 'last

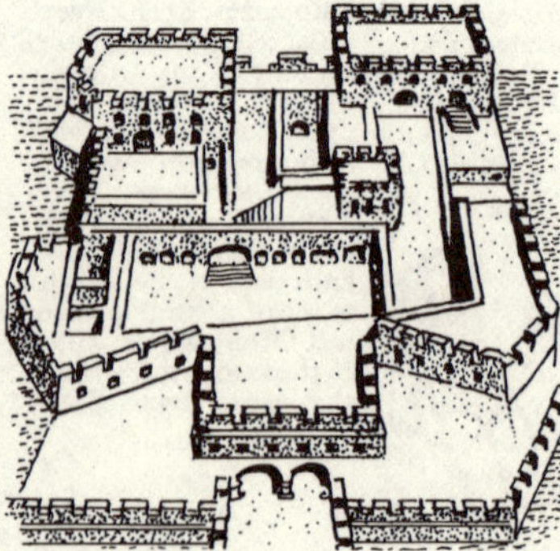

supper' in holy communion/breaking of bread (*see* ☙ 3).

Trials of Jesus Jesus was first tried by the high priest and a group of council members. This trial, held at night on the eve of a festival, was illegal, and so was the calling of witnesses. Those called did not agree with each other, nor were there any defence witnesses. The Jewish leaders said that Jesus was guilty of blasphemy, a crime which carried the death penalty. Early in the morning he was tried by the Sanhedrin – the chief council, or supreme court, of seventy-one Jewish leaders. They were in a hurry to see Jesus put to

Flogging After the death sentence had been passed, it was customary for the prisoner to be flogged with a whip which had small pieces of lead or bone tied to its leather thongs. Jesus was whipped before being crucified.

Crown of thorns Near Jerusalem there were several different kinds of thorny plants from which the crown of thorns may have been made for Jesus.

Resurrection appearances
Jesus appeared to:
1 Mary Magdalene (*John 20*) and 'the other Mary' (*Matthew 28*).
2 Simon Peter (*Luke 24.34*).
3 Two people on the way to Emmaus (*Luke 24*).
4 The disciples – apart from Thomas (*John 20*).
5 The disciples – including Thomas (*John 20*).
6 Seven disciples (*John 21*),
7 Over five hundred of his followers (*1 Corinthians 15*).
8 James (*1 Corinthians 15*).
9 His disciples (*Acts 1*).
10 Paul (*Acts 9*).

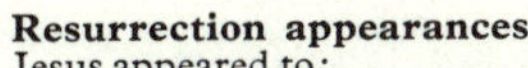

7 Pilate questions Jesus (Jn 18.33–38) **8** Jesus said: "No one takes my life away from me. I give it up of my own free will." (Jn 19.28–30) **9** The guarded tomb (Mt 27.62–66) **10** Surprise for Mary (Jn 20.11–18) **11** Surprise for the disciples (Jn 20.19–23) **12** My Lord and my God (Jn 20.24–29)

death, but before this could happen they needed the Roman Governor, Pontius Pilate, to confirm their sentence. Knowing that Pilate would be more willing to do this for a charge of treason, the Jewish leaders changed their charge.

Burial customs Wealthy people were, whenever possible, buried in a family tomb. This could be a natural cave or one specially cut into the rock. It had to be at least three metres square. The body was bound in linen cloths with a mixture of spices, such as myrrh and aloes, then taken to its final resting place on an open cart.

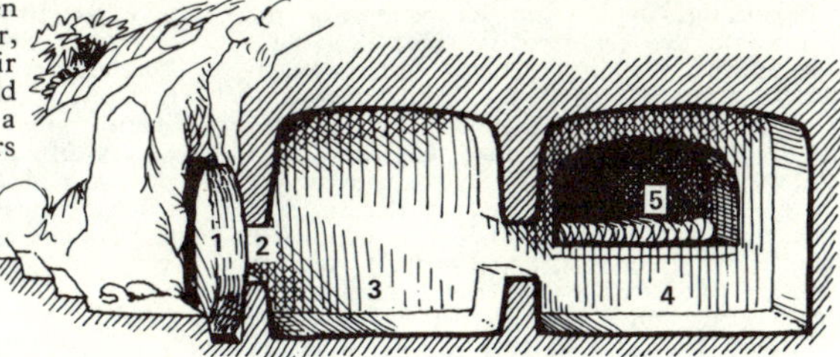

Cross section of a tomb in the rocks: 1 Circular stone door 2 Narrow entrance 3 Outer room 4 Burial room 5 The body was placed in a cavity in the rock wall

Don't forget. Check with the index (*pages 57–63*) for more details on all subjects and Bible references.

The ascension At the end of Jesus' time on earth he returned to be with God his father in heaven (*see* 1).

The fact that he was 'taken up' or 'ascended' does not prove that heaven is located *above* the earth, but simply that it is *away* from the earth in terms of dimension.

Pentecost The Harvest Festival which is called 'Pentecost' or 'day of first fruits', commenced at the end of the barley harvest which had gone on for seven weeks or fifty days. The Greek word 'pentecostos' means 'fiftieth'. At this festival each family had to bring two loaves of bread made from the newly-harvested grain and give them as a special gift to God. The priests offered the bread with the animal and wine offerings. The festival was held for one day (*Sunday*) and kept like a special sabbath: no work to be done and time allowed to worship God.

1 Jesus returns to his Father (Acts 1.6–12)   2 The coming of the Holy Spirit (Acts 2.1–21)   3 Sharing with one another (Acts 2.43–47)   4 Stephen stoned for his faith (Acts 7.54–60)   5 Philip helps an Ethiopian official (Acts 8.26–40)   6 Peter and Dorcas (Acts 9.36–42)

Holy Spirit The Holy Spirit was at work from the beginning, in creation, in inspiring the prophets and the writers of the Old Testament books, and in working through certain individuals for a special event or a limited period of time. The New Testament shows that the Holy Spirit lives in every Christian. He came in a special way to all believers in Jesus at the time of Pentecost (*see* 2). His work is as powerful and unexpected as the blowing of the wind. He brings God's wholeness, or 'Shalom', which is most often translated 'peace' and symbolized by a dove. He guarantees that believers in Jesus shall be completely fit and healthy (whole) in every aspect of their being, and gives them a living relationship with God. The symbol of fire emphasizes the refining power of the Holy Spirit. He 'burns away' all that is wrong and gives 'light' – understanding – of God's way.

Animal food laws The Law (*Leviticus 11*) gives two lists of animals. God's people could eat any from the 'clean' group but none from the 'unclean' group. The animals were separated in this way and labelled 'clean' (*fit to eat*) and 'unclean' (*unfit to eat*) because of their own eating habits and the possibility of spreading disease (*see illus. – unclean animals*). God made these rules for the good of the people – he wanted them to be fit and healthy.

Execution Several methods of execution are mentioned in the Bible. Stoning was used for cases of blasphemy and for certain other crimes. The witnesses for the prosecution had to throw the first stone. Some of the early Christians died for their faith in various ways. Stephen was stoned and James, the brother of John, was beheaded (*see* 9). Crucifixion, not normally practised by the Jews, was a regular method of execution used by the Romans for captives and slaves and for anyone who threatened the stability of the State and its government.

Roman centurion A centurion, appointed by the general from the ranks, was in charge of up to a hundred soldiers.

Prison In Egypt special places were used as prisons, but as imprisonment was not directed by the Law of Moses there is no mention of them until the time of the kings. Then prison rooms or dungeons were built on to the kings' palaces. In New Testament times whole families could be put in prison for debts. Peter was imprisoned more than once in the Jerusalem prison for encouraging the people to believe in Jesus.

Some prisons had an inner prison, perhaps underground. There the prisoners were put in stocks (*see* 3, *p.26*) as an additional punishment and to make escape even more difficult.

While in Rome, Paul was placed under house-arrest, with a soldier chained to him at all times.

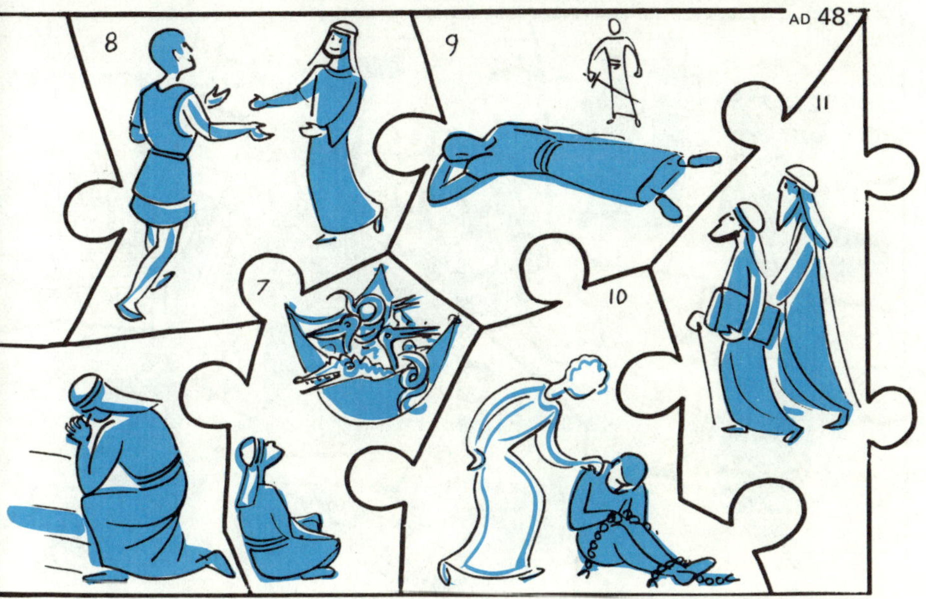

7 A lesson for Peter (Acts 10.9–21) **8** Peter and Cornelius (Acts 10.22–48) **9** Herod Agrippa has James killed (Acts 12.1,2) **10** Peter freed from prison (Acts 12.3–19) **11** An important meeting and an important message (Acts 15.1–35)

The council of Jerusalem As a result of sharing the message of Jesus with people who were not Jews (*Gentiles*), many non-Jews became Christians. A quarrel arose among the Jewish Christians as to whether the Gentiles should be expected to become 'Jews' by following Jewish customs and agreeing to keep the Law. When this matter was discussed at the Council of Jerusalem, it was finally decided that since *God* had obviously accepted these non-Jewish Christians on the grounds of faith alone, then any additions demanded by *men* would only be an unnecessary burden.

Life for the first Christians The first Christians met together daily in the Temple in Jerusalem and in one another's homes. As well as sharing in the Lord's supper together, they met for ordinary meals. But they were ready to share more than just food: many shared their possessions as well, or sold their property to help those in need (*see* 3). The Christian community (*the Church*) grew at a tremendous rate, though before very long they were persecuted for their faith in Jesus and had to leave Jerusalem. But everywhere they went they told others about him and their numbers grew and grew.

Don't forget. Check with the index (*pages 57–63*) for more details on all subjects and Bible references.

Damascus An important centre of communication, Damascus was – and still is – the capital of Syria. While Paul was lodging in Straight Street he received a welcome visit from Ananias.

Ships God's people were not a sea-faring nation: most of their nearest ports were in the hands of alien neighbours (*e.g. the Phoenicians and Philistines*). Even so, they were obviously familiar with sea-going ships and there are many references to these in the Bible. Paul probably used small coastal boats when he went on his missionary travels, but his journey to Rome was made in two of the largest grain ships on their regular run from Egypt to Italy. It was possible for these ships to carry a company of over two hundred crew and passengers.

1 A meeting with Jesus (Acts 9.1–19) **2** A lame man walks again (Acts 14.8–18) **3** Paul and Silas imprisoned (Acts 16.16–40) **4** Sharing the good news in Athens (Acts 17.16–34) **5** Paul defends himself (Acts 22.1–29) **6** Shipwrecked on the way to Rome (Acts 27)

Athens Athens was at the height of her greatness in the fourth century BC, though it remained an important city during New Testament times – under Roman power. It is famous for the hill which dominates the city: the Acropolis, with its temples, statues and monuments. The Parthenon, its most famous building, was a temple to the Greek goddess Athena. Just below this was 'Mars Hill' – the Areopagus – the original meeting place of the ancient court of Athens. It was here that Paul addressed the Greeks.

The Acropolis in Athens: 1 The Parthenon temple 2 Giant statue of Pallas Athena, patron goddess of Athens 3 Two other temples 4 Entrance

Writing materials The most usual material for writing letters on was papyrus – made from the stalks of a tall reed. But it was expensive and not many letters were written. The pen, made from a reed, was sharpened with a knife to a point. Ink – soot mixed with oil or gum and dried in the sun – was moistened with water when required. Rolls, made from sheets of papyrus sewn together, were used for longer letters. The scrolls of the Old Testament were often goatskins, dried and shaped into paper-thin parchment.

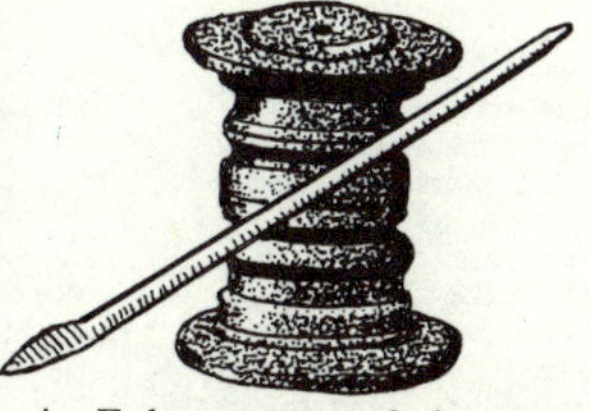

Ephesus The temple of Diana in Ephesus, one of the seven wonders of the ancient world, was four times the size of the Parthenon at Athens and adorned with the works of world-famous craftsmen. An image of the goddess Diana (*Greek: Artemis*) which was claimed to have fallen from heaven, was among the temple's proud possessions. The preaching of Paul and its results caused a big fall in the sales of the little images and figurines, which angered the rich tradesmen.

7 Under house-arrest (Acts 28.16–31) **8** One body with many parts (1 Cor 12.12–31) **9** A complete change (2 Cor 5.17–21) **10** Are you ready? (1 Thes 4.13—5.11) **11** Faith and action go together (James 2.14–18)

Rome, religion In first century Rome the old gods began to lose their attraction with the people. Into the vacuum came varied superstitions and mystery cults: 420 temples in Rome itself were given over to idolatry. The emperors increasingly demanded to be worshipped as gods, so making support of the State a religious duty.

Altar of the Temple of Vespasian

Slavery In Bible times slavery was a common practice. People became slaves in various ways: by capture in war; by purchase in the market place; by birth – the children of slaves automatically became slaves themselves; as punishment for theft or to work off a debt; to avoid starvation – the poor sometimes sold themselves as slaves rather than die of starvation. The Romans used slaves for the running of their homes, for sport (gladiators who fought one another and wild animals), for building (roads and fine houses) and for rowing large galley ships.

Some of the wealthy Jews had servants: *bondservants* who belonged to their master and were usually well-treated; *ordinary servants* who worked under the bondservants; then perhaps some *hired servants* found in the market place.

The return of Jesus This is clearly promised in the Bible: the Lord Jesus Christ will return in power and glory; he will raise the dead; gather together his people; demonstrate God's justice to the nations and finally destroy all evil.

Don't forget. Check with the index (*pages 57–63*) for more details on all subjects and Bible references.

John on Patmos

John, the disciple of Jesus, wrote the book of *Revelation* when he was an old man and a prisoner for his faith.

At a time when Christians were being persecuted, and even killed for their faith, John was sent from his home (possibly at Ephesus) to the island of Patmos.

Revelation was probably written as a circular letter and taken by a messenger to the seven churches.

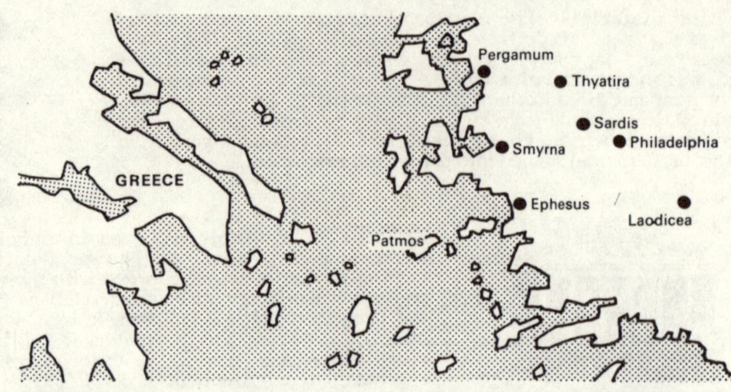

1 God is light (1 Jn 1.5–10)   2 Love one another (1 Jn 4.7–21)   3 Island of Patmos (Rev 1.9–11)
4 Seven churches represented by seven lamps (Rev 1.12–20)   5 Jesus at the door (Rev 3.14–22)   6 Throne of God (Rev 4)

Writing style The writing style of *Revelation* is the style that was used in times of persecution. Much of the book is written in a kind of code language. It makes plain the difference between good and evil, God and Satan, light and darkness. Although it spoke to the people to whom it was written, it also points forward to the time when God will bring in a new order. God will be seen as the victor over evil and those who have been faithful to him will be rewarded.

Seals Thousands of engraved seals from the Ancient Near East, including Israel, have been found. Cylinders, rings and stamps were used as a mark of authority or to witness a document. To secure a document a scroll was often tied by a cord that had a clay seal fixed to it. The scroll could be read only when the seal had been broken by a person in authority. A sealed book or prophecy meant it was still unrevealed (*see* 7).

Heaven An actual description of heaven is not given in the Bible, but it does give some idea of what the term means. Heaven is the place where God is. Thus to be in heaven is to be with God in a closer way than can be experienced now. The Christian can look forward to this after death.

The Bible also uses the words 'the heavens' to refer to the space above the earth. The 'new heaven and new earth' point to a time when the world as it is now will be replaced by God's new order, where everyone loves and obeys him.

The last judgement The Bible speaks of a final judgement which everyone will have to face. God is the Judge and he will restore perfect justice. His judgement is perfect because he is a God of love and holiness. All will be judged according to the truth God has made available to them, on the basis of their faith in Jesus Christ and the life they have lived. Judgement needs to be taken seriously, but the Christian need not be afraid.

Hell The term is used to describe the condition of final and total separation from God. It results from his judgement on all evil. But people can be saved from judgement by faith in Jesus Christ for the forgiveness of their sin.

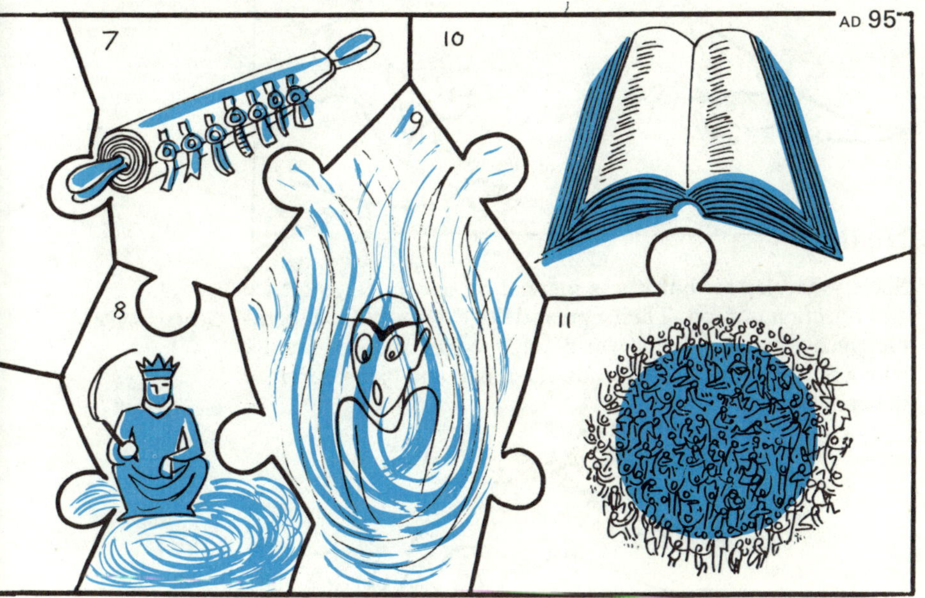

7 The unopened scroll (Rev 5)　　**8** Harvest time (Rev 14.14–20)　　**9 & 10** Final judgement (Rev 20.7–15)
11 The new heaven and the new earth (Rev 21.1–4)

The bride Marriages were usually arranged by parents. The engagement took place in the girl's home when she was about twelve. It was a solemn promise made by the engaged couple before witnesses. The parents of the bridegroom promised to give the bride and her parents some money, and they usually gave their son a present as well. A marriage gift would be given to the girl by her parents. The bridegroom's gift to the bride was often jewellery and clothes. The engagement was so important that the couple could not change their minds, and if the man died before the wedding day, the woman was regarded as a widow.

The wedding took place about a year after the engagement. The bride was dressed in the finest clothes the family could afford and had a necklace of coins. The bridegroom came to the girl's home to collect his bride, and the bride and her bridesmaids went out to meet him. A torchlight procession took them to the bridegroom's house for the wedding celebrations, which lasted for about a week.

John describes 'the Holy City, the new Jerusalem' as 'a bride dressed to meet her husband'.

Don't forget. Check with the index (*pages 57–63*) for more details on all subjects and Bible references.

God and his people

In the beginning GOD . . .

The first words in the Bible are an introduction to God the Creator of the universe. What he made, he loved completely. Mankind was able to have a relationship with him: freely and fully to love him, one another and his world. But the people God created refused the demands of love. They rejected God when they disobeyed him; and life in its completeness was lost. Hatred, violence and death became realities; but God's love continued.

Genesis 1.1

Genesis 1.26–28

Genesis 3

Genesis 4.1–6

Noah

Society developed: but it was marked by selfishness, violence and rejection of God. Then a great deluge, sent by God, completely overwhelmed the world: only Noah and his family, with a representation of all kinds of animals and birds, survived to begin again.

Genesis 6.9–22

Genesis 9.8–17

Abraham

God wanted a people (nation) who would live in such a distinctive relationship with him that every other nation would see how trusting him brought wholeness to life. He called Abraham and promised that his descendants would become a nation and that through them *all* nations would see God's special care.

Abraham trusted the Lord and his relationship with God was made right.

Genesis 12.1–3

Romans 4.13

Moses

But Abraham's descendants did not carry out the Lord's plan. They did not understand that his people had been chosen for a purpose or mission. Moses was given the task of leading the Israelites out of Egypt and of teaching them what it meant to be a distinctive people of God. They were to love and worship him only and to live in a way that honoured and pleased him.

Deuteronomy 10.12–22

Exodus 19.3–6

Exodus 20.1–17

A land for the people of God

The Lord gave his people a land. Again and again he reminded them of what was expected of them, but they ignored his words and went their own way. They refused God's love and kingship and wanted to become like the surrounding nations. They imagined that a visible king would lead them to victory in their battles.

Deuteronomy 7.1–11

Judges 2.11–19

1 Samuel 8.4–22

David and Solomon

Israel's first king, Saul, openly disobeyed the Lord's commands, but when God chose David he promised that one of his descendants would become a king who would rule with justice and whose Kingdom would last for ever.

2 Samuel 23.1–5

2 Samuel 7.16

In spite of many failings, King David loved God throughout his life. He was always ready to thank the Lord for his goodness.

2 Samuel 7.18–29

Psalm 103

Solomon, David's son, built a magnificent Temple in Jerusalem, and was renowned for his wisdom. Yet the time came when he turned away from God and built temples for the gods of other nations.

1 Kings 9.1–9

Proverbs 1.1–19

1 Kings 11.1–13

Two kingdoms

After the death of King Solomon, the kingdom was divided
into two – Israel and Judah. Instead of attracting the nations
to the true God, the Lord's people were attracted to the false
gods of the surrounding nations. Religious practices in both
Israel and Judah became a sham and meant nothing to God. Amos 5.21–24
He hated their sacrifices and holy days because of their lying Micah 3.1–3, 8–12
and cheating, their mistreatment of the poor and the cor- Amos 5.10–15
ruption in the courts. God had urged his people to be distinctive, like him – loving and seeking justice in all they said
and did – but they constantly refused to be the kind of people
he wanted. This hurt and grieved him: yet still he loved them.
He sent his prophets to warn them of their wrongdoing and to Jeremiah 3.19–22
call them to be different; but they ridiculed God's messengers Jeremiah 4.1–4
and threw his prophet Jeremiah into prison. Jeremiah 18.18
Jeremiah 37.11–21

Because they would not change, God allowed Israel and Judah Hosea 7.8–16
to be defeated and taken to Assyria and Babylon, as he had 2 Kings 21.9–15
warned. God spoke to the Jews who had been taken to Babylon
and told them to seek the well-being of others – even of the Jeremiah 29.4–7
Babylonians.

As God promised, Judah eventually returned to the land they Zephaniah 3.14–20
had been given. Isaiah 43.1–21

The Lord's Servant

God chose Israel to serve him and to show his justice and Isaiah 43.10
power to the nations, but Israel failed him. Isaiah, the prophet, Isaiah 49.3
foretold the day when God's Servant would come and succeed Isaiah 52.13—53.12
where Israel had failed. This Servant, descended from David,
would come as 'Prince of Shalom' (*see page 24*) to bring in Isaiah 9.6,7
God's Kingdom of justice and to restore his world to wholeness. Isaiah 11.1–5
Our 'shalom', or wholeness, would come through his Isaiah 53.4–6
sufferings.

When Jesus came, he claimed to be the Servant that God had Matthew 12.15–21
promised. Luke 4.16–19

Jesus the Son of God

Jesus was born to Mary and grew up as part of a family. As he got older he observed life closely and stored away all he knew about God. He learnt how to understand people – their needs and the way they lived.

Matthew 1.18–25
Mark 6.1–4
Luke 2.40–52

When Jesus was anointed by the Holy Spirit he set out to show the world what God's reign or Kingdom really is: forgiveness, freedom, justice, joy and togetherness. Many of his parables give illustrations of what God's reign is like, and his actions (*miracles*) are signs that God's reign can be seen in Jesus. Other powerful signs are the resurrection of Jesus, the gift of the Holy Spirit and the creation of the loving, new family of his disciples. These events make God's Kingdom real.

Romans 14.17
Parables and miracles listed on pages 62 and 63
1 Corinthians 15.12–22
John 16.5–15
John 15.9–17

The death and resurrection of Jesus

Through the death and resurrection of Jesus, God made it possible for his creation to be restored to complete wholeness. When Jesus is seen and accepted as Saviour a new relationship with God begins. Those who believe in Jesus Christ become God's children. They are called to be like him and the Holy Spirit makes this possible. When he takes control of a child of God, he gives him the power to show the world what it means to belong to the family of God; and God's Kingdom grows.

Romans 3.21–26
Colossians 1.19–22
Ephesians 1.4,5
Romans 8.14–17
Galatians 4.4–7
Galatians 5.16, 22–26
Ephesians 1.22, 23
Colossians 1.17, 18

Family of God

God's family is bound together by love – a special love which must be seen and shared outside the family. It is God's love for his children, their love for him and for one another. Together they praise God and do his work, looking forward to the return of Jesus when the whole of God's family will be with him, and God will reign as King for ever.

1 John 4.7–21
1 John 3.16–18
John 15.9–17

How we got the Bible

God could have dictated it word for word . . . but he did not.

Men might have tried to think it up . . . but that wasn't what happened.

God wanted us to have a reliable book about himself. He chose a variety of people from many different backgrounds to write it. The books that they wrote say what God wanted them to say because the Holy Spirit helped them and made sure they got it right.

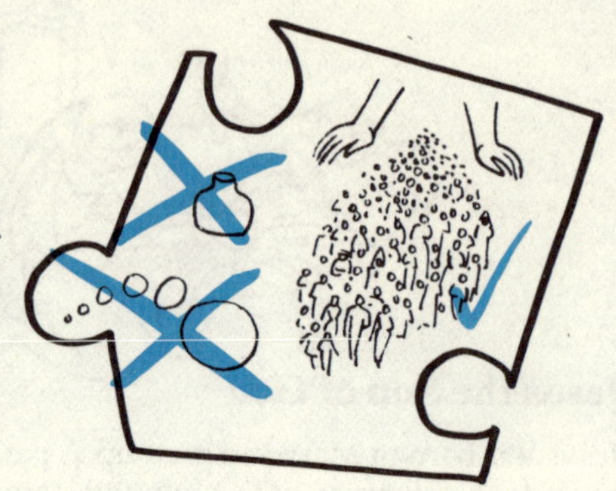

The Bible has 66 different books, written by at least 39 different authors over a period of some 1500 years, yet it all fits together to give a true picture of God.

The books that were written have been translated into different languages and passed on from one generation of Christians to the next.

All the Old Testament was written before Jesus was born and the books collected together from very ancient accounts.

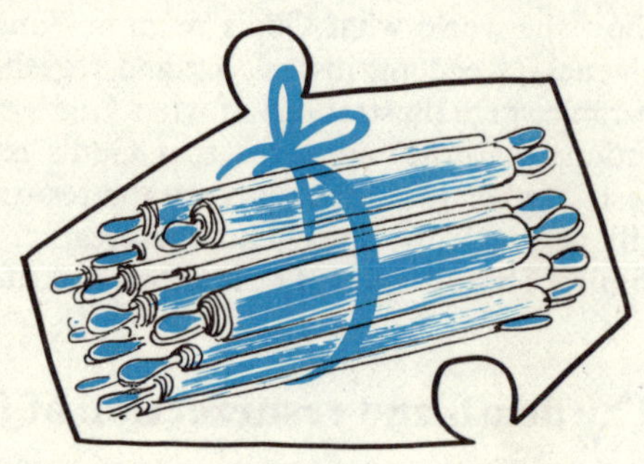

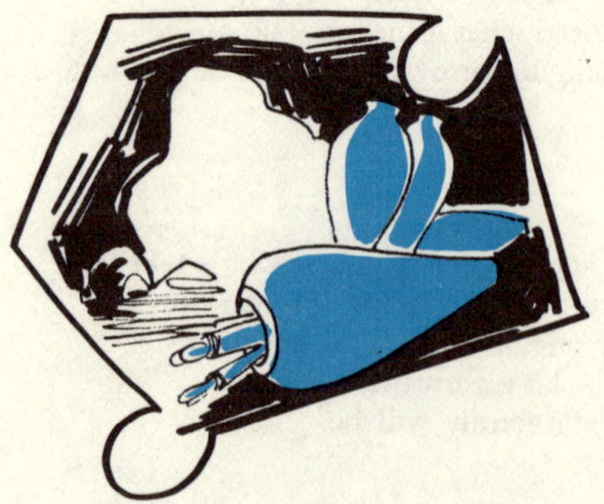

Scrolls, containing fragments of most Old Testament books, were discovered in the Dead Sea area in 1947. They probably date from the last few centuries BC and the earlier part of the first century AD, and are the oldest manuscripts available.

Nearly all the Old Testament books are mentioned in the New Testament. All the New Testament books were written in the first century AD; copies on papyrus were circulated to the churches.

The earliest almost-complete manuscripts of the Gospels discovered so far date from the third century AD. But there are also fragments from the early part of the second century. All these were found in Egypt.

Constantine, a Roman emperor, became a Christian in AD 312 and commanded that many copies of the Bible should be written on parchment. This meant that more churches could have a copy of the Bible.

From the ninth century thousands of manuscripts have survived – written in Greek, Latin, Syriac and other languages.

At first every manuscript was copied out by hand; then came the printing revolution and the Bible was far more readily available. From the Reformation, many people could read it for themselves for the first time.

1488 First printed Hebrew Old Testament

1516 First printed Greek New Testament

1526 New Testament first translated into English by William Tyndale

1535 The whole Bible translated into English by Coverdale

1611 King James Version

1881 Revised Version

Some modern translations

1946 and 1952 Revised Standard Version

1958 and 1964 Amplified Bible

1961 and 1970 New English Bible

1966 and 1976 Today's English Version; Good News Bible

Can we trust the Bible?

The Bible is a book that claims to be true:

'All Scripture is inspired by God and is useful for teaching the truth . . .' (*2 Timothy 3.16*)
Many of the historical events and customs have been backed up by the findings of archaeologists.

Very old copies of the Bible have been found – much older than the earliest manuscripts of ancient writers such as Homer, Virgil and Plato.

The Bible is a book that is true:

- It contains true facts about God and how to find him.
- It contains true facts about people and events.
- It contains stories which tell the truth in a vivid way.

Countless numbers of people – rich and poor, clever and not so clever – have believed that the Bible is true and their lives have been changed.

We can know the Bible is true because:

- God the Father who gave his Word is truth.
- God the Son – Jesus Christ – came to show the truth, and he said that God's Word is true.
- God the Holy Spirit is 'the Spirit who reveals the truth about God'. He inspired the writers and opens 'closed' eyes to see the truth about God's Word. He shows people how to live as true Christians and helps them to stand up for what they know is true.

What is it all about?

The Bible is not . . .

a history textbook – though it is full of historical events
a science handbook – though it talks of subjects studied by scientists
a geography manual – though every nation's history is influenced by its geographical situation and character
a philosophical work – though questions of philosophy are introduced
a literary masterpiece – though it contains some beautiful writing

The Bible is . . .

a book about God – and what he is like
a book about people – and the kind of people God wants us to be and the kind of life he wants us to lead.

The Bible doesn't simply teach certain facts, like a school textbook; it does something no other book can do. It gives God's own words, introduces him to the reader and helps the reader to get to know him. It speaks of Jesus Christ the Saviour and shows how contact can be made with him – and so with God himself. And this is the best thing that can happen to anyone.

It is the life of Jesus Christ which divides the Bible into two: the Old Testament looks forward to his arrival and prepares for it; the New Testament tells of his life, death and resurrection, showing how they deal with the problem of sin. It makes plain how a new life is possible for those who believe in Jesus Christ when the Holy Spirit comes to live in them and transform them into God's people.

History and Law

The word 'Pentateuch' means five scrolls. These begin with creation; then follows the story of God's people from Abraham to Moses. God's rules for life and worship are given throughout the five books – one of the simplest statements being the ten commandments.

History

The history of God's people is traced from their entry into Canaan to the overthrow of the two kingdoms – Israel and Judah – to their time as captives in foreign lands, and their eventual return home.

Life stories of men and women form the framework of these books. Leaders, prophets and priests emphasize the importance of a true relationship with God.

Poetry and Wisdom

Biblical poetry uses repetition and rhythm to make a passage easy to remember. When it uses repetition, sometimes the second phrase or line adds thoughts on the same theme (*Isaiah 55.8,9*), and at other times the second line expresses a contrast to the first (*Psalm 1.6*). The musical rhythms of the psalms make them suitable for singing.

Proverbs, riddles, popular sayings, parables and allegories can all be found in the wisdom literature. The books of poetry and wisdom give vivid and important instructions on how to live, and warnings of what will happen if they are ignored.

Prophecy

Prophets, men called by God to speak for him to his people, explain the *past*, recalling God's law and his promises; they speak against the evils of the *present*; they declare the *future* – what God is going to do. Although their message often tells of punishment and doom, they sometimes glimpse the hope of the future – the coming Messiah and a new relationship with God.

Biography and History

The four Gospels are not just historical records. They are also portraits of Jesus as the Messiah or Christ. The writers present the good news, and encourage their readers to believe in Jesus, God's Son. Although they write a few decades after the death of Jesus, eye-witnesses still lived to testify to the events and the spoken tradition, both of which are used as a basis for the Gospels. Acts covers the thirty years following the birth of the Church at Pentecost and charts its growth through the lives of Peter and Paul.

Letters

The letters are written to individuals, churches or groups of churches. They deal with the 'teething problems' of the early Church. The basic teaching is about God the Father, Jesus Christ (God the Son), God the Holy Spirit, and living as a Christian. Some letters can be dated as early as AD 50, but they were all written before the end of the first century.

Prophecy

The book of Revelation looks forward to the final triumph of God and the reign of the Lord Jesus Christ. To convey this message John uses symbolic language, as did some of the Old Testament prophets before him.

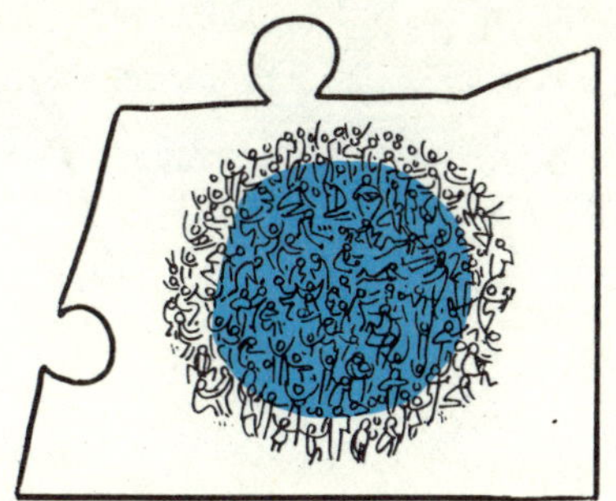

How to read and understand the Bible

Different kinds of books have to be read in different ways. A textbook has to be studied and remembered; a light novel can be skipped and still enjoyed. But the Bible, because it is different from any other book, has to be read in a special way.

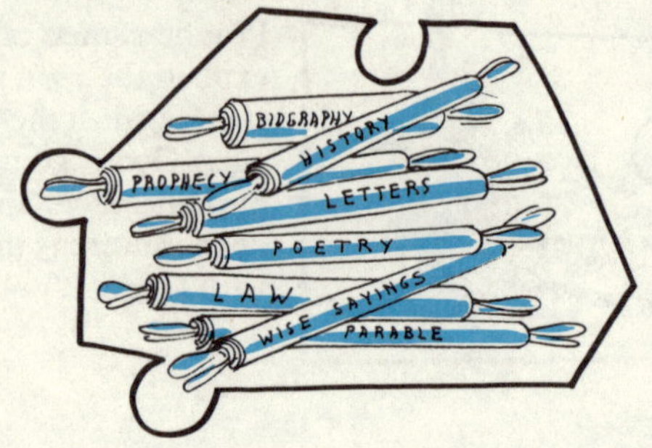

When and where you read it is not important, but make sure you find the best place for you.
- You can read and think alone.
- You can read and discuss with others.
- You can learn from other people who have studied the Bible and live by its teaching.

Remember God wants to speak to you through the Bible, and the Holy Spirit will help you to understand it.

The Bible was written for people of every time and every place, so look first for the plain and obvious meaning. Because the writer of each book had particular people and places in mind when he wrote, it also helps to find out:
- when, where and by whom it was written
- why it was written
- in what style it was written – history, biography, law, poetry, wise sayings, prophecy, parable or letter
- the meaning of the words for the people who first read them
- what the verses mean when compared with the whole story and (*sometimes*) with other parts of the Bible.

But the most important question to ask is: 'What is God saying to me today and what must I do about it?'

that God will help you to understand and learn from what you read.

some Bible verses from the book you are working through.

- What have I read about God the Father, the Lord Jesus Christ, or the Holy Spirit?
- Is there a command to obey?
- Is there a promise to believe?
- Is there a good example to follow?
- Is there a wrong thing I should avoid?
- What have I learnt from my reading?

Pray that God will help you to act on what you have learnt.

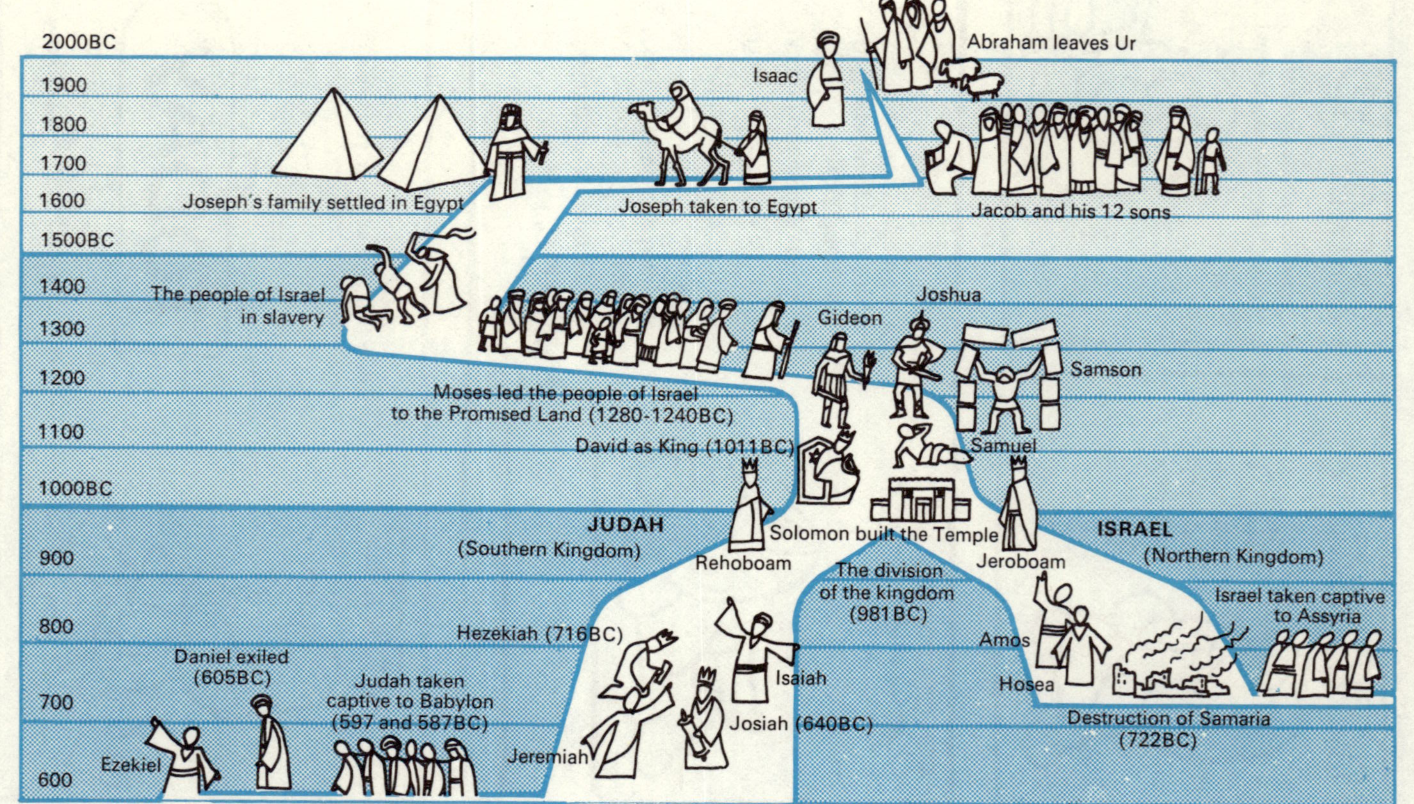

2000BC
1900
1800
1700
1600
1500BC
1400
1300
1200
1100
1000BC
900
800
700
600
Abraham leaves Ur
Isaac
Jacob and his 12 sons
Joseph taken to Egypt
Joseph's family settled in Egypt
The people of Israel in slavery
Moses led the people of Israel to the Promised Land (1280-1240BC)
Joshua
Gideon
Samson
Samuel
David as King (1011BC)
Solomon built the Temple
The division of the kingdom (981BC)
JUDAH (Southern Kingdom)
ISRAEL (Northern Kingdom)
Rehoboam
Jeroboam
Amos
Hosea
Hezekiah (716BC)
Isaiah
Josiah (640BC)
Israel taken captive to Assyria
Destruction of Samaria (722BC)
Daniel exiled (605BC)
Judah taken captive to Babylon (597 and 587BC)
Jeremiah
Ezekiel

Time Check from Abraham to Jesus

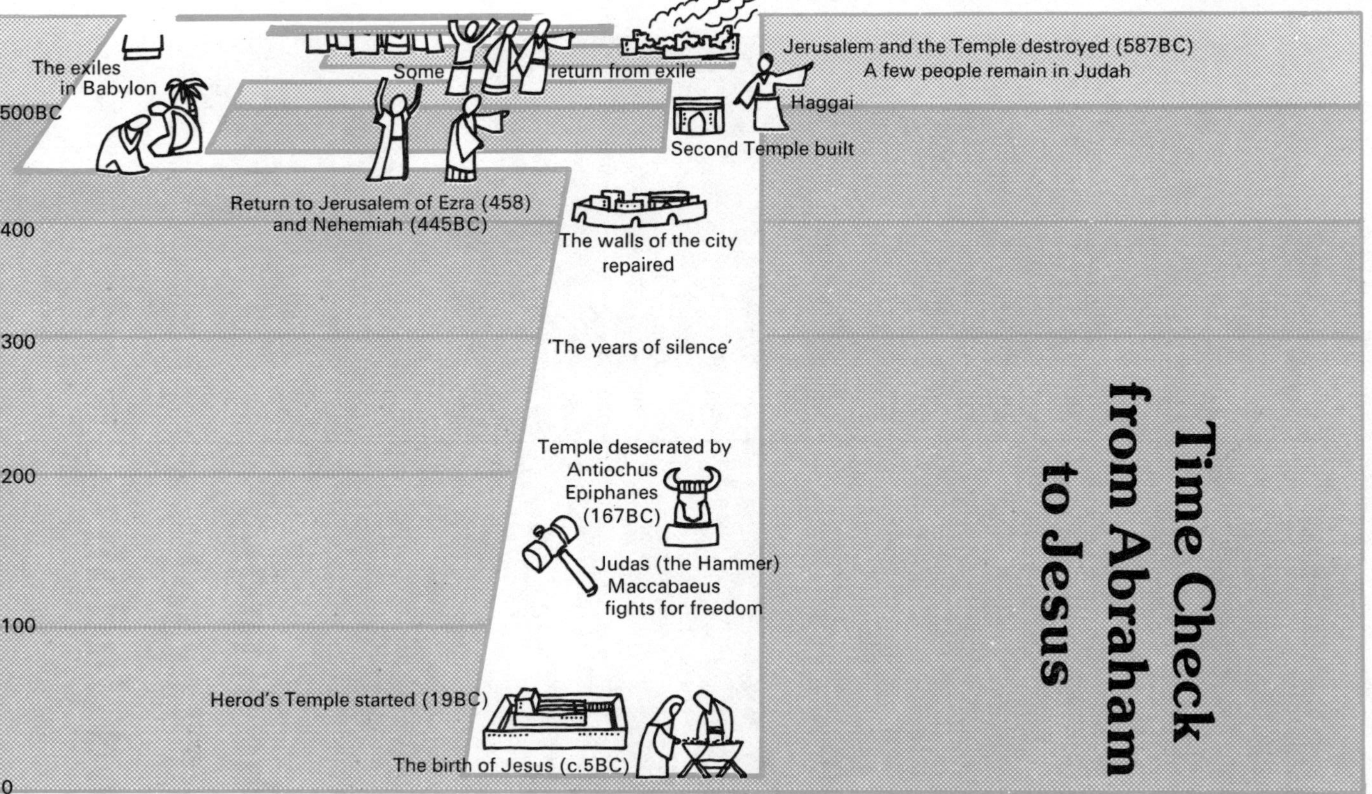

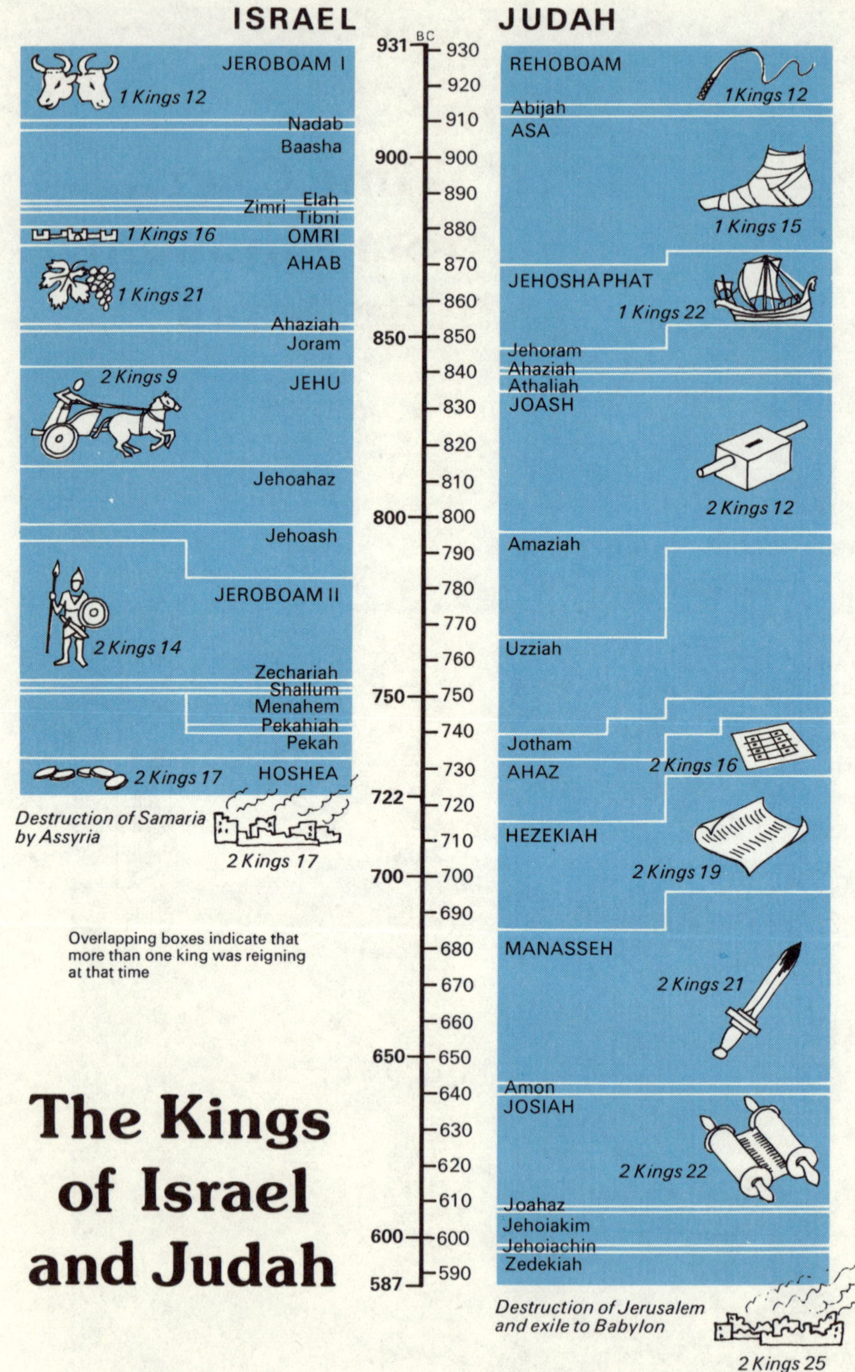

The Kings of Israel and Judah

The Jewish Calendar

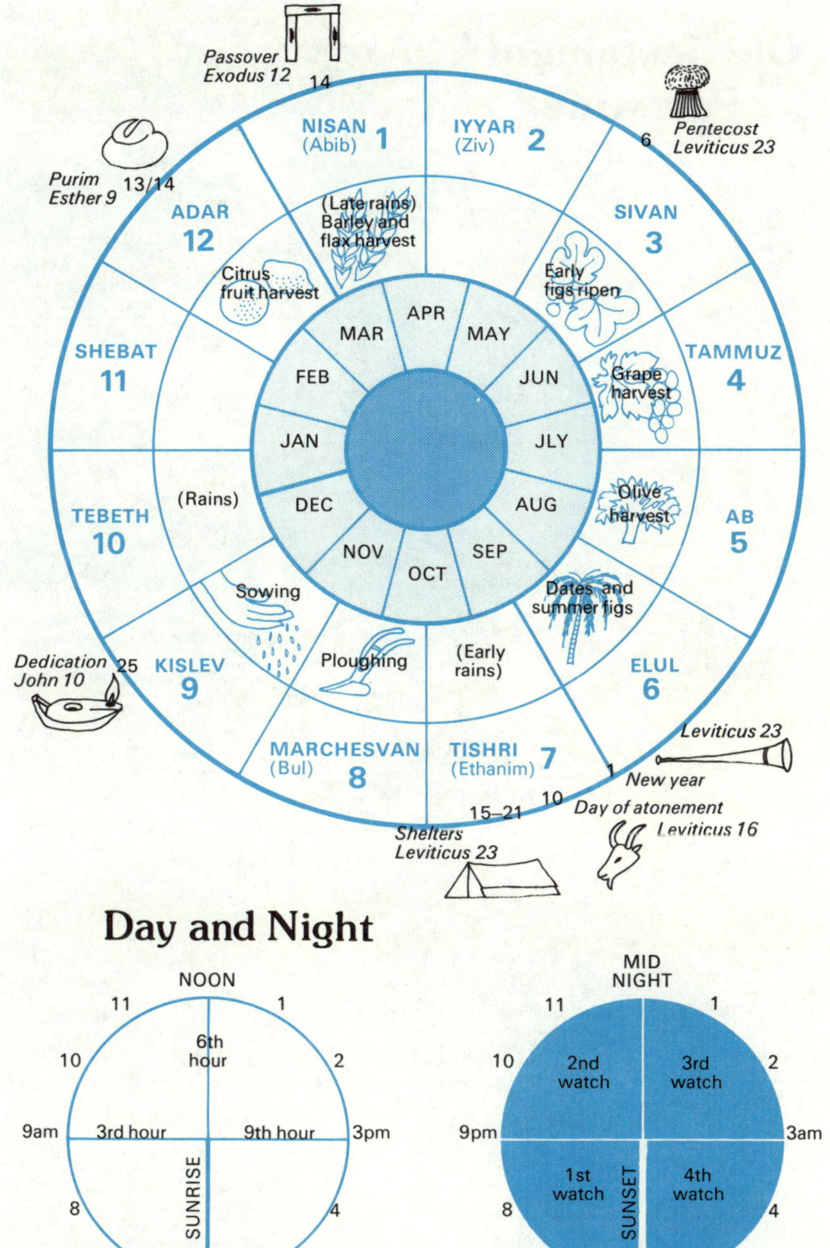

Day and Night

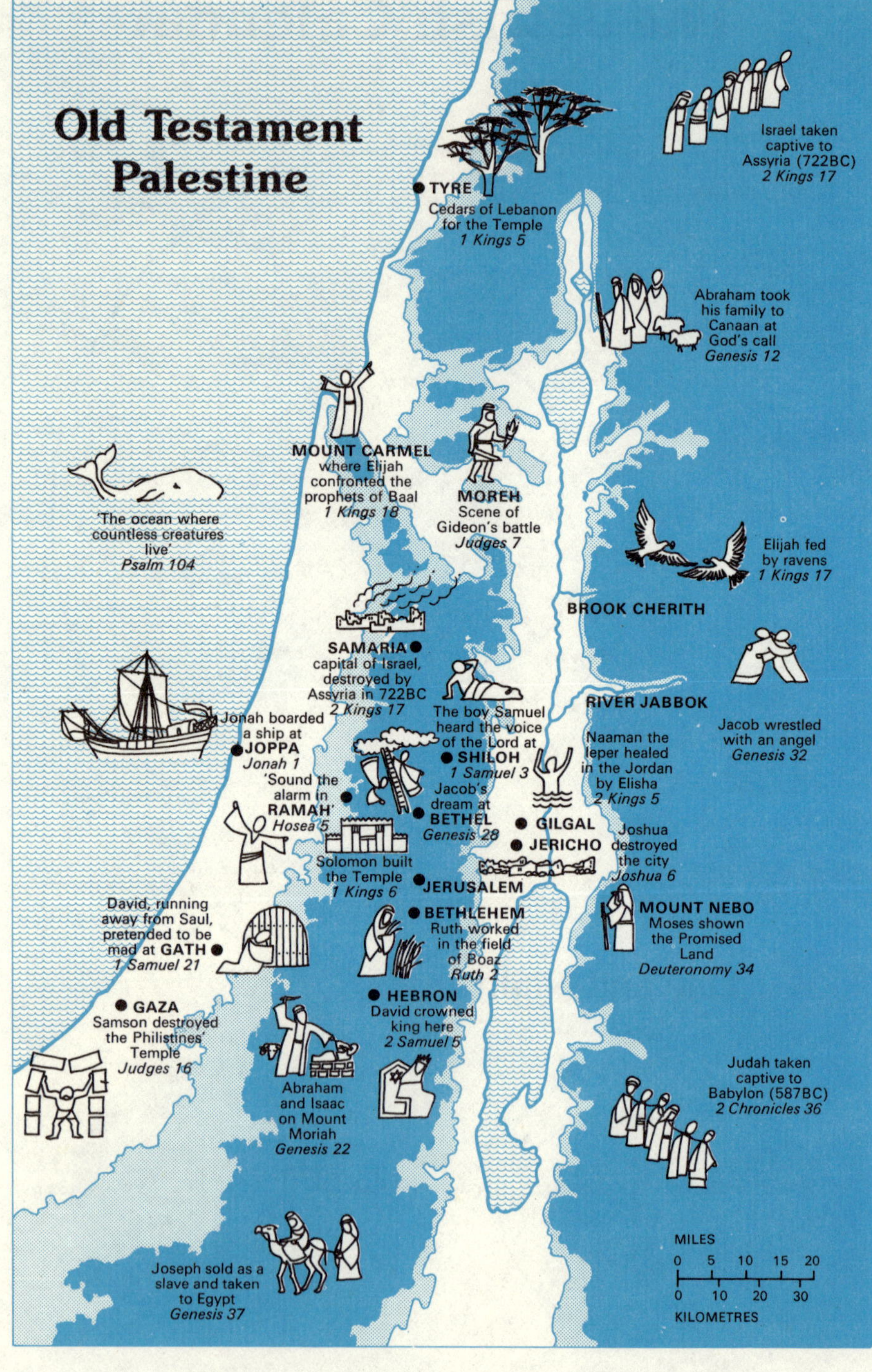

Old Testament Palestine
TYRE
Cedars of Lebanon for the Temple
1 Kings 5
Israel taken captive to Assyria (722BC)
2 Kings 17
Abraham took his family to Canaan at God's call
Genesis 12
MOUNT CARMEL
where Elijah confronted the prophets of Baal
1 Kings 18
MOREH
Scene of Gideon's battle
Judges 7
'The ocean where countless creatures live'
Psalm 104
Elijah fed by ravens
1 Kings 17
BROOK CHERITH
SAMARIA
capital of Israel, destroyed by Assyria in 722BC
2 Kings 17
The boy Samuel heard the voice of the Lord at
RIVER JABBOK
Jacob wrestled with an angel
Genesis 32
Jonah boarded a ship at
JOPPA
Jonah 1
SHILOH
1 Samuel 3
Naaman the leper healed in the Jordan by Elisha
2 Kings 5
'Sound the alarm in
RAMAH'
Hosea 5
Jacob's dream at
BETHEL
Genesis 28
GILGAL
JERICHO
Joshua destroyed the city
Joshua 6
Solomon built the Temple
1 Kings 6
JERUSALEM
David, running away from Saul, pretended to be mad at GATH
1 Samuel 21
BETHLEHEM
Ruth worked in the field of Boaz
Ruth 2
MOUNT NEBO
Moses shown the Promised Land
Deuteronomy 34
GAZA
Samson destroyed the Philistines' Temple
Judges 16
HEBRON
David crowned king here
2 Samuel 5
Abraham and Isaac on Mount Moriah
Genesis 22
Judah taken captive to Babylon (587BC)
2 Chronicles 36
Joseph sold as a slave and taken to Egypt
Genesis 37
MILES
0 5 10 15 20
0 10 20 30
KILOMETRES

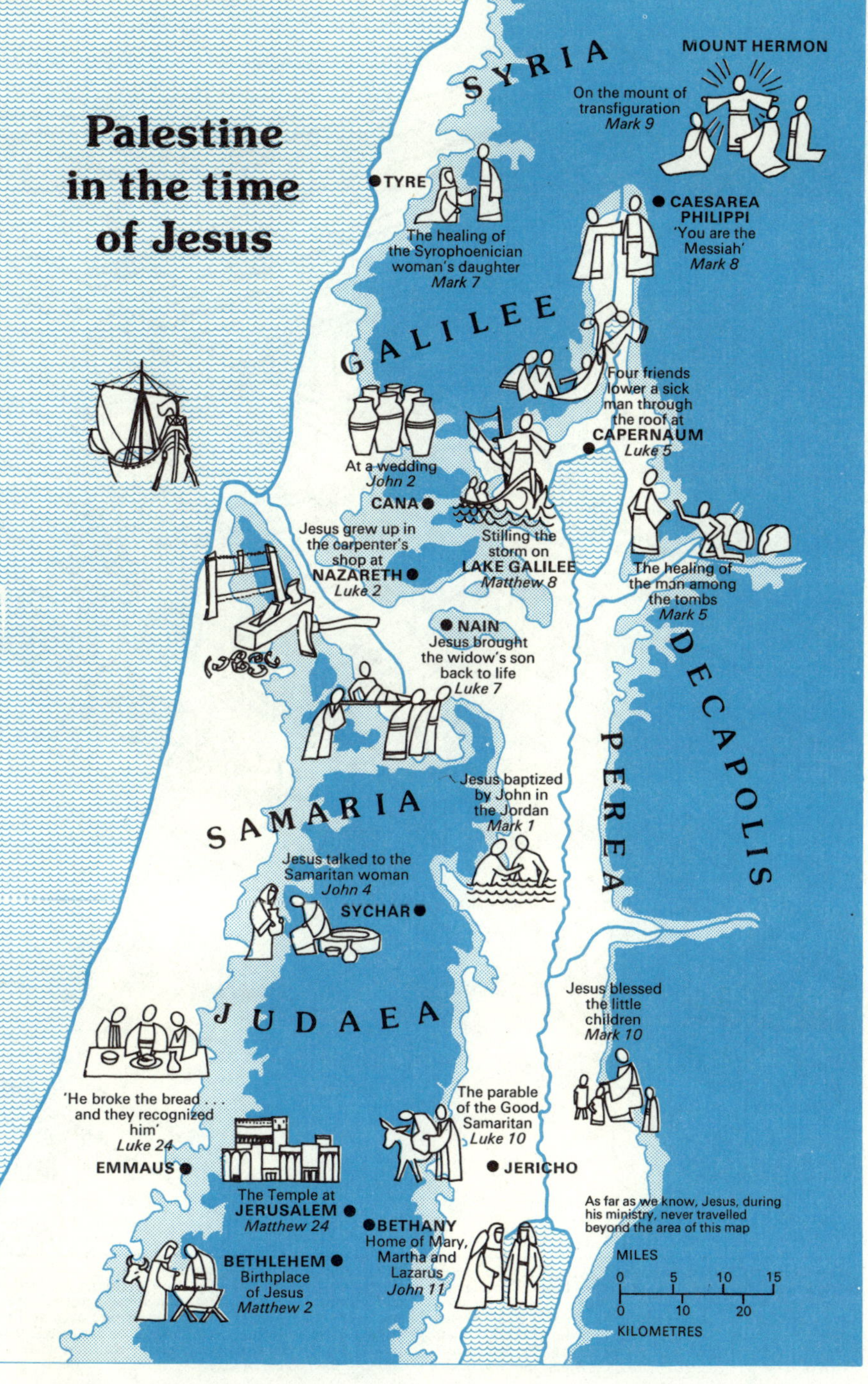

Palestine in the time of Jesus
SYRIA
MOUNT HERMON
On the mount of transfiguration
Mark 9
TYRE
The healing of the Syrophoenician woman's daughter
Mark 7
CAESAREA PHILIPPI
'You are the Messiah'
Mark 8
GALILEE
Four friends lower a sick man through the roof at
CAPERNAUM
Luke 5
At a wedding
John 2
CANA
Jesus grew up in the carpenter's shop at
NAZARETH
Luke 2
Stilling the storm on
LAKE GALILEE
Matthew 8
The healing of the man among the tombs
Mark 5
DECAPOLIS
NAIN
Jesus brought the widow's son back to life
Luke 7
SAMARIA
Jesus baptized by John in the Jordan
Mark 1
PEREA
Jesus talked to the Samaritan woman
John 4
SYCHAR
Jesus blessed the little children
Mark 10
JUDAEA
'He broke the bread . . . and they recognized him'
Luke 24
EMMAUS
The parable of the Good Samaritan
Luke 10
JERICHO
The Temple at
JERUSALEM
Matthew 24
BETHANY
Home of Mary, Martha and Lazarus
John 11
As far as we know, Jesus, during his ministry, never travelled beyond the area of this map
BETHLEHEM
Birthplace of Jesus
Matthew 2
MILES
0   5   10   15
0   10   20
KILOMETRES

Jerusalem in Old Testament times: King Solomon carried out the building of the first Temple in Jerusalem. When the project was begun a platform of stone levelled and enlarged the site. All the stone was quarried nearby from deep underground, then dragged there, shaped and ready to use, by thousands of men. The workmen (1) dragged the stone blocks up ramps made of rubble, sand and clay (2). These were the type of ramps used by the Egyptians for building the pyramids. Scaffolding and some ramps (3) were made of wood, but it was scarce in that area and only used where a lighter structure was required. Logs, placed under the stone, provided primitive wheels for moving the largest blocks.

Workmen lifted the heavy bronze columns into place (4). First, they were probably dragged up a ramp on to the Temple platform, then raised with blocks of wood – placed underneath them – to a height from which they could be pulled up with strong ropes. Other teams of men steadied the columns until they were safely in position.

Mules and oxen – not as plentiful as men – may have been used to transport objects like the bronze tank (5), the twelve bronze bulls that the tank rested on (6) and the altar for the sacrifices (8). As the wood was ready to use, the carpenters only had to put it in position (7).

Jerusalem in New Testament times: looking over the old city to Herod's Temple. This Temple was erected on the same site as the one built by Solomon.

Various festivals were held throughout the year, but the one most looked forward to was the Festival of Shelters (*Tabernacles*). It was a harvest thanksgiving held for a week; a time when the people rested from their work, praised God and brought their gifts. They also remembered the journey of their ancestors from Egypt to Canaan. Every family built a shelter to live in

for the whole week. They varied from fairly substantial huts to small shelters of leaves and rushes put up in the streets. Some were built on the roofs of the houses. Makeshift beds or mattresses were taken from the houses for sleeping on.

It was a time of music, of singing and dancing. Streets were crowded with happy, laughing people. Soldiers on patrol saw that order was kept.

Jesus in Jerusalem

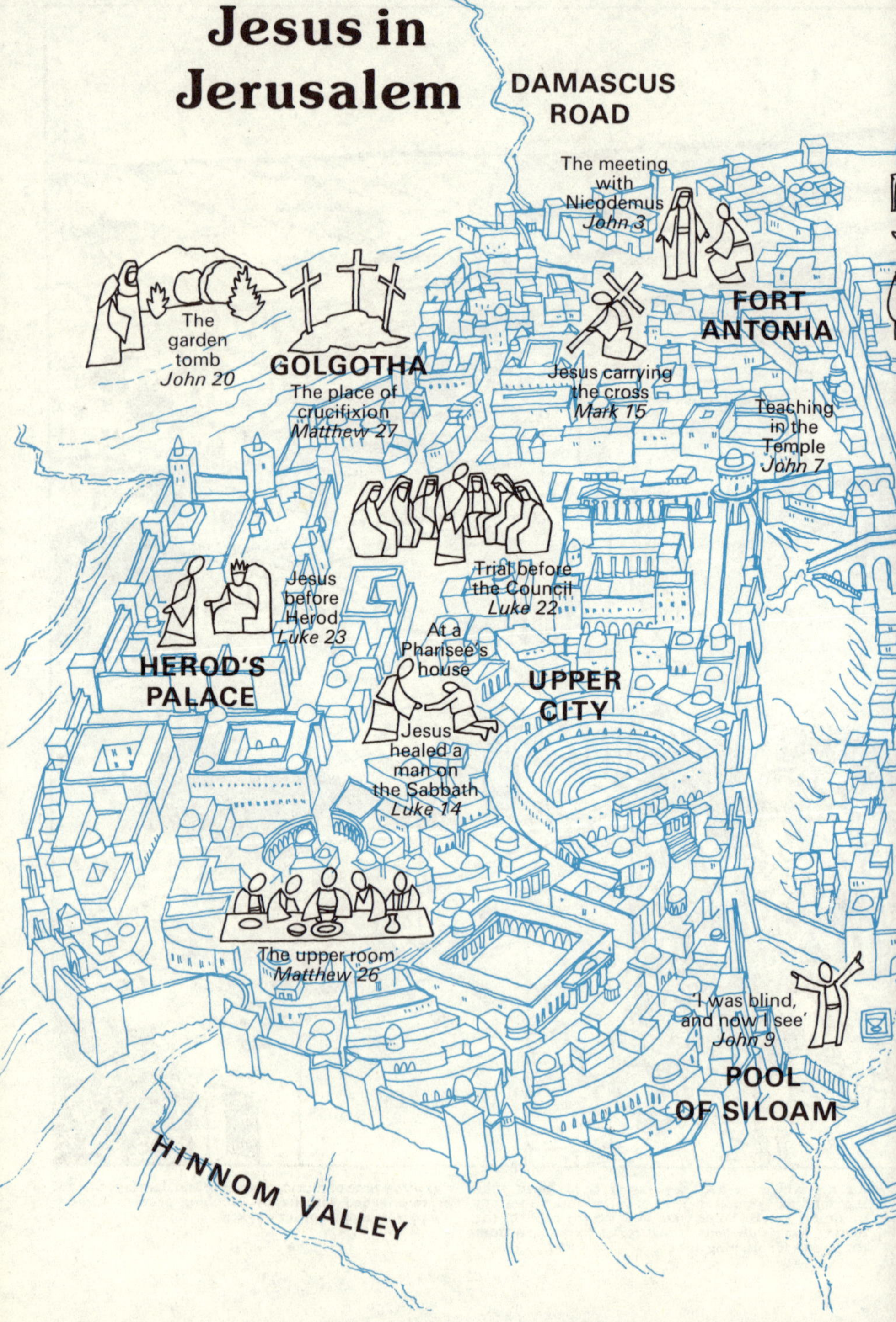

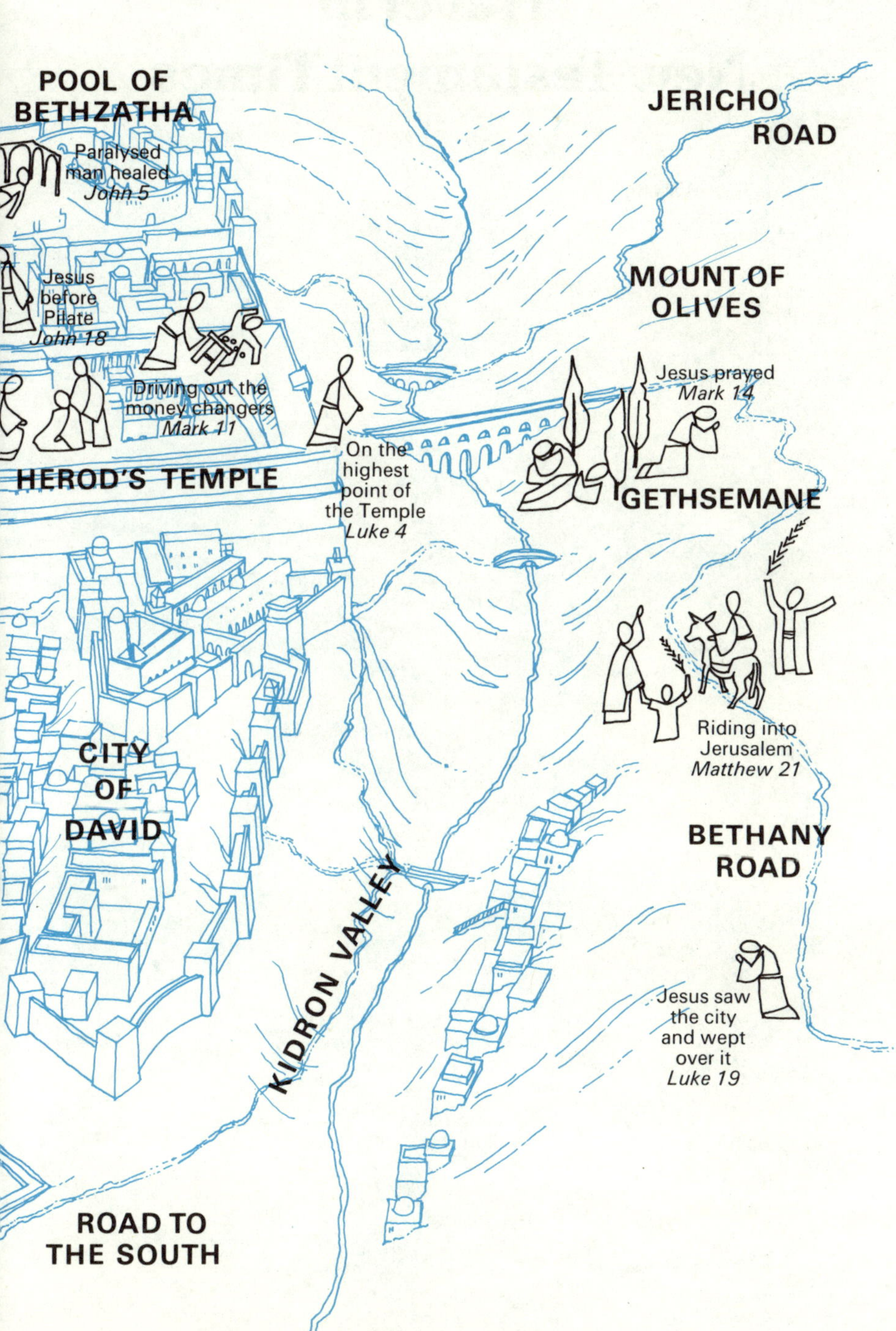
POOL OF
BETHZATHA
Paralysed man healed
John 5
Jesus before Pilate
John 18
Driving out the money changers
Mark 11
HEROD'S TEMPLE
On the highest point of the Temple
Luke 4
JERICHO ROAD
MOUNT OF OLIVES
Jesus prayed
Mark 14
GETHSEMANE
Riding into Jerusalem
Matthew 21
BETHANY ROAD
CITY OF DAVID
KIDRON VALLEY
Jesus saw the city and wept over it
Luke 19
ROAD TO THE SOUTH

Travel in New Testament Times

Paul's Missionary Journeys

First

Second

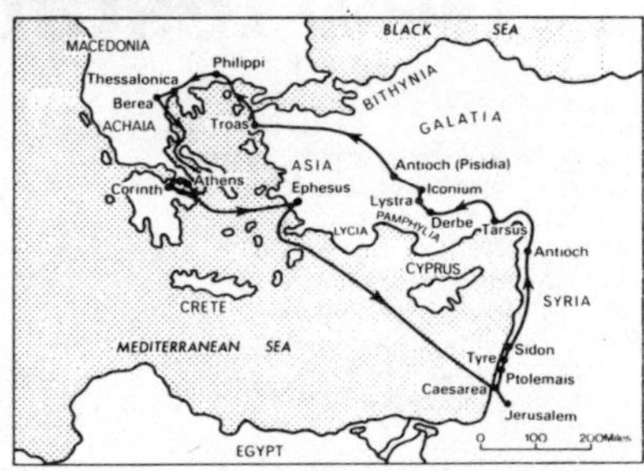

Third

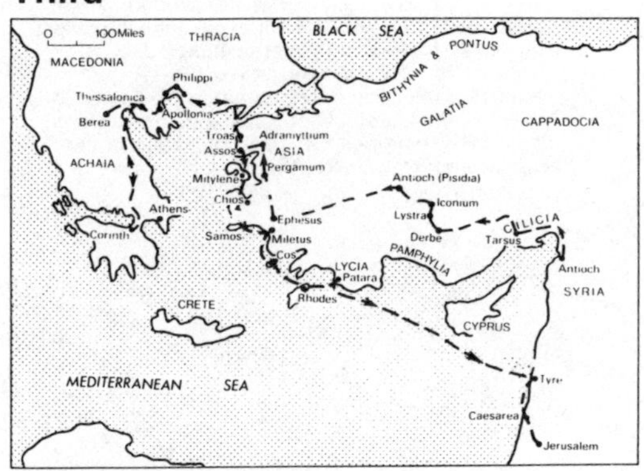

Travelling is something that is taken for granted these days, but in New Testament times it was extremely slow, difficult, and even dangerous. However the spread of the Roman Empire forced the need for good communications. Their road building was so good that there is still some to be found in existence today !

It took nearly two months to travel by land from Rome to Caesarea, while today, by aeroplane, it takes something like two hours. In the light of this the amount of travelling done by Paul and his friends is amazing.

Voyage to Rome

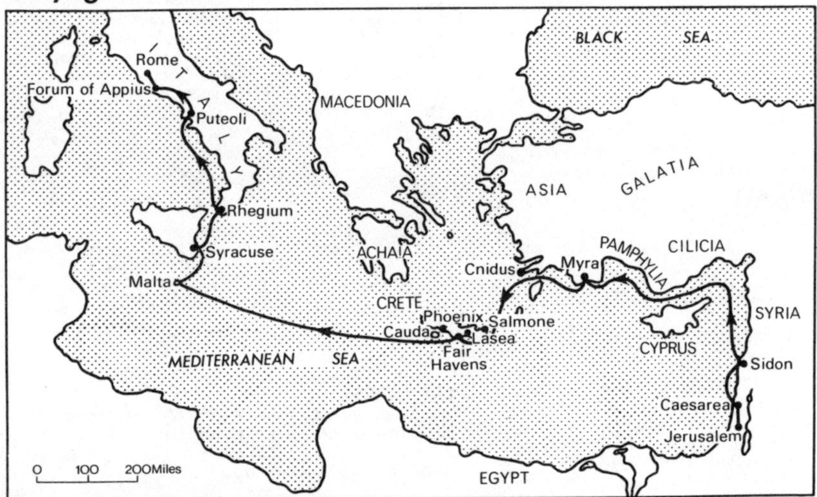

Money in New Testament Times

Coins circulated in Palestine from three main sources. The Imperial money from Rome, provincial money from Tyre and Antioch (Greek coinage), and Jewish money possibly minted at Caesarea. It is not surprising that money-changing was big business *(see John 2.14–15).*

THE ASSARION
A Roman bronze coin, worth 'two sparrows' *(see Matthew 10.29).* There were 16 assarions to the denarius.

THE TETRADRACHMA

THE SHEKEL AND HALF–SHEKEL

THE JEWISH LEPTON
Referred to as 'little copper coins' in the Good News Bible, they were of low value – but see the story of the widow's 'mites' in *Luke 21.3.*

THE ROMAN DENARIUS
The commonest silver coin of the New Testament. It was a day's wage for a working man *(Matthew 20.2).* The Samaritan gave the innkeeper two denarii for looking after the injured Jew *(Luke 10.35).* This was the coin of Caesar that Jesus used to confound his enemies *(Luke 20.24).* The equivalent Greek coin was the silver *drachma,* which in the parable probably formed part of the bride's headdress *(Luke 15.8).*

THE ROMAN STATER
Judas was paid 30 'silver coins' for betraying Jesus *(Matthew 26.15).* These could have been either the Roman *stater* or the Greek *tetradrachma,* each worth four denarii. The *half-shekel* temple tax for *two* people could be paid with this coin *(see Matthew 17.27).*

THE TALENT
In the parable *(Matthew 25.14–30)* the master distributes to three servants gold Greek coins, each worth nearly 1000 silver *minas* (GNB silver coins) or 1500 silver *staters.*

FIND OUT MORE!

This index is more than an index. It will help you to find your way around the Bible Guide, but it also gives some Bible references for you to look up. If you turn to all the pages listed and check with the Bible references given, you will discover a great deal more about each topic.

Key
Example: Building **p12p48p49**p13(9)p15(11): Bible references; *see also* Houses, Temple
● The pages listed in bold type at the beginning refer to paragraphs about the subject or to maps or charts in the Bible Guide: **p12p48p49**.
● Then the jigsaw pieces are listed: p13(9) p15(11).
● Abbreviations of Bible books: check with the list of Contents at the front of your Bible.
● *see also* Houses, Temple: look up these entries as well to find out more information.

A

Abraham *see* Tents **p7**, Covenants **p9**, Altars **p10**p6(4): Gen 11.27–25.11; Lk 16.19–31; Jn 8.31–58; Acts 7.1–8; Rom 4.1–25; Gal 3.6–29; Heb 11.8–12,17–19; Jas 2.21–24
Alexander the Great p16p16(1)
Altars p10p9(9)p12(4): Gen 8.20; 22.9; Ex 17.15; 1 Kgs 1.50–53; 18.30–35; Mt 5.23,24
Angels p18 p7(7)p18(1)p25(10): Ex 23.20–23; Ps 103.20; Mt 4.11; Lk 1.8–20, 26–38; Acts 12.6–10; Heb 1.4–7,13,14
Animal food laws *see* Food laws
Anointing p10p10(1)p18(5): Ex 29.4–7; 30.22–33; 1 Sam 10.1; 16.1,13; 1 Kgs 19.15,16; Lk 4.18,19; Jn 1.32–34; Acts 10.38; 1 Jn 2.20,27
Antiochus Epiphanes p16p16(4)
Ark (Box) of the Covenant *see* Covenant box
Ascension *see* Jesus Christ
Assyria p14p14(1): enemies of Israel 2 Kgs 15.19,20,29; 18.9–12; enemies of Judah 2 Kgs 18.13–19.37; judgement against Assyria Is 10.12
Athens *see* Cities
Augustus, Emperor of Rome p17p17(8): Lk 2.1

B

Bride p29p6(5)p29(11): Gen 24.1–67; Ps 45.10–17; Prov 31.10–31; Is 49.18; 61.10; Eph 5.21–33; Rev 21.2
Building p12p48p49p13(9)p15(11): Gen 4.17; Ex 1.11; Deut 22.8; Josh 24.13; 2 Chr 26.9,10; Neh 2.17,18; 3.1–4.23; Amos 7.7; Mt 7.24–27; Lk 12.16–21; 2 Cor 5.1; Col 2.6.7; *see also* Houses, Temple
Burial customs p23p21(11)p23(10): Gen 23.1–20; 50.1–14,26; Ps 79.1–4; Mt 27.57–61; Lk 7.11–15; Jn 19.38–42

Babies p18p18(2): Lk 2.7
Babylon p15 captives taken to Babylon p14(5): 2 Kgs 25.18–21; fall of Jerusalem 2 Chr 36.11–21; judgement against Babylon Jer 25.12–14
Bible pp34–41: Ex 24.12; 34.27; Ps 102.18; 119.1–176; Is 30.8; 40.8; Jer 30.1,2; Jn 20.30,31; Gal 3.8; 2 Tim 3.16,17; Heb 4.12; 2 Pet 1.21
Birthright p7p6(6): Gen 25.31–34; 27.1–29; 2 Kgs 2.9; 1 Chr 5.1; Heb 12.16,17

C

Canaan p31 (A land for God's people): Gen 10.6,15–19; 37.1; Num 13.17–20,25–33; Ps 105.10,11; Mt 15.21–28; *see also* Canaanite religion
Canaanite religion p9: Num 25.1–5; Judg 2.11–13; 6.25–32; 1 Kgs 18.16–40; 2 Kgs 10.18–28; 2 Chr 33.1–17; 34.3–7; Jer 19.1–9
Carpenter p21: Ex 31.1–5; 2 Chr 2.8,9; Is 44.13–20; Mk 6.1–3
Centurion (Officer) p25p25(8): Mt 8.5–13; Mk 15.39,44,45; Acts 10.1–48; 22.22–29; 27.1,42–44
Cities
 Alexandria *see* Writing: Greek Old Testament **p16**p16(3): Acts 6.8,9; 18.24–26; 27.6
 Athens p25p26(4): Acts 17.16–18.1; 1 Thes 3.1–5
 Damascus p26: Gen 15.2; 1 Kgs 20.34; 2 Kgs 5.12; Is 8.3,4; Acts 9.1–25; Gal 1.15–17
 Ephesus p27: Acts 19.1–20.1,17–38; 1 Cor 16.8,9; Eph 1.1; 1 Tim 1.1–3; Rev 1.9–11; 2.1–7
 Rome, religion **p27**: Acts 2.10; 23.11; 28.16; Rom 1.1–7; 2 Tim 1.16,17
Clothes p13p7(8)p8(2): Gen 37.3,23,31–34; Ex 3.5; 39.1–31; Deut 24.10–13; Is 3.16–24; Mt 6.25–34; Jn 19.23,24; Acts 9.36–42; 1 Pet 3.1–6; Rev 7.13,14
Coming of age p18p18(3): Lk 2.42; *see also* Early learning
Council of Jerusalem p25p25(11): Acts 15.1–31; verdict of council 15.19,20,23–29
Covenant p9
 Noah p30p6(3): Gen 6.18; 9.8–17
 Abraham, Isaac and Jacob p30p6(4)p7(7): Gen 12.1–3; 15.1–6,18; 17.1–14; Ex 2.23–25; Ps 105.7–11
 Phinehas: Num 25.10–13
 David p31: 2 Sam 7.8–16

Maps and charts
pp42–43 Time chart – From Abraham to Jesus
p44 Kings of Israel and Judah
p45 Seasons
p46 Old Testament Palestine
p47 Palestine in the time of Jesus
pp48–51 Scenes in Old and New Testament Jerusalem
pp52–53 Jerusalem in the time of Jesus
pp54–55 Travel and Paul's journeys
p56 Coins

Miracles p20p8(2 to 5)p9(8)p12(3,6) p13(7,8)p15(7 to 9)p19(7,9,10)p20(3,4)p21 (8,11)p23(10 to 12)p24(6,10)p26(2)p27(9) : Ex 3.1–3; 14.5–30; 16.1–36; 17.1–7; Josh 6.1–21; 1 Kgs 17.1–24; 2 Kgs 2.11; 4.11–37; 5.1–14; Dan 3.8–30; 5.1–31; 6.1–24; Mk 16.20 (see full list of miracles of Jesus **p62**); Acts 3.1–10; 9.36–43; 14.8–10; 2 Cor 5.17–19

Moses p30p8(1 to 7) : in Egypt Ex 2.1–14.31; in the desert 15.22–18.27; at Sinai Ex 19.1–33.1; 34.1–35; the books of Leviticus, Numbers, Deuteronomy; Mt 8.4; 17.3,4; Lk 20.37; Jn 3.14; Acts 7.20–44; 28.23; Heb 3.1–6; 11.23–28; Rev 15.2–4; *see also* Disasters of Egypt, Egyptian slave-drivers, Tent of the Lord's Presence

Musical instruments p11p9(8)p10(2,4)p15 (11)p27(10) : 1 Sam 16.14–23; 1 Kgs 1.39,40; 1 Chr 25.1–8; 2 Chr 5.11–14; 7.6; Ps 137.1–6; 150.1–6; Dan 3.5; Mt 9.23; 1 Cor 13.1; Rev 18.22

N

Noah p6p30p6(3) : Gen 5.28–9.29; Is 54.9; Ezek 14.12–14; Mt 24.37–39; Heb 11.7; 1 Pet 3.18–22; 2 Pet 2.5; *see also* Flood, Other flood stories

P

Parables of Jesus p20p21(9,10) : Mt 13.10–16; see full list of parables **p63**
Passover *see* Festivals, *see also* Disasters (plagues) of Egypt
Pentecost *see* Festivals, Holy Spirit
Pharisees p17p17(6)p20(5) : Mt 3.7–9; 9.9–14,32–34; 12.1–8,14; 15.1–9,12–14; 16.1,6,11,12; 22.34–46; 23.1–33; 27.62–66; Lk 7.36–50; 16.14,15; 18.9–14; Jn 3.1; 7.32,45–52; Acts 5.33–39; 15.5; 23.6–9; *see also* Sadducees
Philistines p11p10(3) : Gen 21.34; Judg 3.1–6; 10.6,7; 14.1–4; 15.1–16.1; 1 Sam 4.1–6.18; 13.3–7; 14.1–23; 17.1–54; 31.1–13; Ezek 25.15–17; Amos 1.6–8
Plagues *see* Disasters (plagues) of Egypt
Ploughing and sowing p21 : Gen 47.23,24; Lev 25.1–7; Deut 8.7; 22.10; 1 Kgs 19.19–21; Job 4.8; Mt 13.1–9,18–23; Mk 4.26–29; Lk 9.62; Gal 6.7–9

Prison p25p25(10)p26(3) : Gen 39.19–23; 40.1–23; Judg 16.21; 1 Kgs 22.26,27; Jer 32.1–5; 40.1–6; Mt 14.3–12; 27.15–26; Acts 5.17–42; 12.1–19; 16.16–40; 2 Tim 1.8; Heb 13.3
Prophets p12p10(1)p12(1,3,4,6)p13(7 to 11) p14(4,6)p15(8,9)p18(4,5) : Deut 18.14–22; 34.10–12; 1 Sam 9.6–11; 10.5–7; 1 Kgs 12.21–24; 13.1–32; 17.1; 2 Kgs 2.1–18; Is 6.1–13; 30.8–11; Jer 1.4–19; 14.14,15; Amos 7.10–17; Mt 7.15–20; 22.37–40; Lk 11.29,30; Jn 4.19; Acts 7.37,38; 10.43; Heb 1.1; 1 Jn 4.1–3
Ptolemies p16p16(2)

R

Resurrection appearances of Jesus *see* Jesus Christ
Return of Jesus *see* Jesus Christ
Rome *see* Cities

S

Sabbath p20p8(6)p21(8) : Gen 2.1–3; Ex 20.8–11; Neh 13.15–22; Amos 8.5,6; Mt 12.9–14; Mk 2.23–28; *see also* Synagogue
Sacrifice p10p9(9)p11(11)p12(4)p23(8) : Gen 4.3–5; 8.20–22; 22.1–19; Ex 29.38–42; Lev 1.1–7.38; 16.1–28; 1 Kgs 18.36–39; Ps 50.7–14,23; Amos 5.21–24; Mal 1.6–14; Jn 1.29; Rom 12.1–3; 1 Cor 5.7; Heb 9.23–28; 10.1–18; 1 Pet 1.18–21; *see also* Altars, Antiochus Epiphanes, Maccabean revolt
Sadducees p17p17(6) : Mt 3.7–9; 16.1,6,11–12; 22.23–32; Acts 4.1–3; 5.17; 23.6–10; *see also* Pharisees
Samaritans p14p15(12)p20(1)p21(9) : 2 Kgs 17.24–41; Ezra 4.1–6; Lk 9.51–56; 10.25–37; 17.11–19; Jn 4.1–30,39–42; Acts 1.8; 8.9–25
Scrolls *see* Writing
Seals *see* Writing
Second coming *see* Jesus Christ (Return)
Seleucids p16p16(2,4)
Sennacherib p14p14(1) : 2 Kgs 18.13–19.37; 2 Chr 32.1–23; Is 36.1–37.38
Septuagint (Greek Old Testament) *see* Writing
Servant of the Lord *see* **p32**
Servants p27p6(5)p13(8)p22(4) : Gen 24.1–67; 2 Kgs 5.1–4; Is 41.8–10; Mt 8.5–13; 18.21–35; Mk 10.43–45; Jn 15.15; Rom 1.1; Col 3.22–24; Jas 1.1; 2 Pet 1.1; 2.18–21; *see also* Servant of the Lord
Shepherds and sheep p10p18(2) : Ps 23.1–6; Is 40.10,11; 53.6,7; Ezek 34.1–31; Zech 11.4–17; Mt 9.35–38; Lk 2.8–20; 15.1–7; Jn 10.1–16; Heb 13.20,21; 1 Pet 5.1–4

MIRACLES OF JESUS

Healing of individuals	Matthew	Mark	Luke	John
Son of government official				4.46–54
Sick man at a pool				5.1–18
Man in synagogue		1.21–28	4.31–37	
Man with skin-disease	8.1–4	1.40–45	5.12–16	
Roman officer's servant	8.5–13		7.1–10	
Dead son of a widow			7.11–15	
Peter's mother-in-law	8.14,15	1.29–31	4.38,39	
An uncontrollable man		5.1–20	8.26–39	
Paralysed man	9.1–7	2.1–12	5.17–26	
Woman with severe bleeding	9.20–22	5.25–34	8.43–48	
Dead girl	9.18–26	5.21–43	8.40–56	
Dumb man	9.32–34			
Man with a paralysed hand	12.9–14	3.1–6	6.6–11	
Blind and dumb man	12.22		11.14	
Canaanite woman's daughter	15.21–28	7.24–30		
Deaf and dumb man		7.31–37		
Blind man at Bethsaida		8.22–26		
Boy with epilepsy	17.14–18	9.14–29	9.37–43	
Blind Bartimaeus		10.46–52	18.35–43	
Woman with a bad back			13.10–17	
Sick man			14.1–6	
Man born blind				9.1–41
Dead friend named Lazarus				11.1–44
Slave's ear			22.47–51	
Healing of groups				
Crowd in Capernaum	8.16,17	1.32–34	4.40,41	
Two blind men	9.27–31			
Crowd by Lake Galilee		3.7–12		
Crowd on the hillsides by Lake Galilee	15.29–31			
Ten men			17.11–19	
Control over laws of nature				
Water changed into wine				2.1–11
Catch of fish			5.1–11	
Jesus calms a storm	8.23–27	4.35–41	8.22–25	
Great crowds (5,000 men alone) are fed	14.13–21	6.30–44	9.10–17	6.1–13
Jesus walks on the water	14.22–33	6.45–52		6.16–21
Great crowds (4,000 men alone) are fed	15.32–38	8.1–10		
A fish and the payment of taxes	17.24–27			
Fig tree withers away	21.18–22	11.12–14, 20–24		
Another catch of fish				21.1–11
Christ conquers death	28.1–10	16.1–11	24.1–12	20.1–18

SOME PARABLES AND ILLUSTRATIONS OF JESUS

	Matthew	Mark	Luke	John
About nature and farm life				
Birds and flowers	6.25–34		12.22–31	John never
A tree and its fruit	7.15–20		6.43–45	speaks about
The sower	13.1–9	4.1–9	8.4–8	parables
Growing seed		4.26–29		but he does
Unfruitful fig tree			13.6–9	use common
Weeds	13.24–30, 36–43			things and everyday life
Mustard seed	13.31,32	4.30–32	13.18,19	to point to
Lost sheep	18.10–14		15.1–7	truths about
Workers in the vineyard	20.1–16			God and
Tenants in the vineyard	21.33–46	12.1–12	20.9–18	God's world
Fig tree	24.32–35	13.28–31	21.29–33	
Sheep and goats	25.31–46			
Harvest time				4.35–38
The shepherd				10.1–18
Grain of wheat				12.20–26
The vine				15.1–17
About familiar things in Bible times				
Water				4.5–14 7.37–39
Salt	5.13	9.50	14.34,35	
Light	5.14–16	4.21,22	8.16–18 11.33–36	8.12
Bread				6.25–35
House builders	7.24–27		6.46–49	
Patching clothes	9.16	2.21	5.36	
New wine	9.17	2.22	5.37–39	
Yeast	13.33		13.20,21	
The pearl	13.45,46			
The fishing net	13.47–50			
Lost coin			15.8–10	
About everyday life				
New truths and old	13.51,52			
Forgiveness	18.21–35			
Two sons	21.28–32			
The wedding feast	22.1–14		14.15–24	
Ten girls at a wedding	25.1–13			
Servants	25.14–30		19.11–27	
Debts and debtors			7.41–43	
Good Samaritan			10.25–37	
Friend in need			11.5–13	
Rich fool			12.16–21	
Watchful servants			12.35–40	
Humility and hospitality			14.7–14	
Counting the cost of discipleship			14.25–33	
Lost son			15.11–32	
Shrewd manager			16.1–13	
Rich man and Lazarus			16.19–31	
A servant's duty			17.7–10	
The persistent widow			18.1–8	
Pharisee and tax-collector			18.9–14	